Avoiding Burnout

**CORWIN
PRESS**

The Corwin Press logo—a raven striding across an open book—represents the happy union of courage and learning. We are a professional-level publisher of books and journals for K-12 educators, and we are committed to creating and providing resources that embody these qualities. Corwin's motto is "Success for All Learners."

Avoiding Burnout

A Principal's Guide
to Keeping the Fire Alive

Barbara L. Brock
Marilyn L. Grady

CORWIN PRESS, INC.
A Sage Publications Company
Thousand Oaks, California

For information:

Corwin Press, Inc.
A Sage Publications Company
2455 Teller Road
Thousand Oaks, California 91320
www.corwinpress.com

Sage Publications Ltd.
6 Bonhill Street
London EC2A 4PU
United Kingdom

Sage Publications India Pvt. Ltd.
M-32 Market
Greater Kailash I
New Delhi 110 048 India

Printed in the United States of America

Library of Congress Cataloging-in-Publication Data

Brock, Barbara L.
Avoiding burnout: A principal's guide to keeping the fire alive /
Barbara L. Brock & Marilyn L. Grady.
    p. cm.
Includes bibliographical references.
  ISBN 0-7619-7806-2
  ISBN 0-7619-7807-0 (pbk.)
  1. School principals—Job stress. 2. Educational leadership—Psychological
aspects. I. Grady, Marilyn L. II. Title.
  LB2831.9 .B76 2002
  371.2′012—dc21

                                                    2002002772

This book is printed on acid-free paper.

02 03 04 05 10 9 8 7 6 5 4 3 2 1

Acquisitions Editor:	Robb Clouse
Associate Editor:	Kylee Liegl
Editorial Assistant:	Erin Buchanan
Copy Editor:	Barbara Coster
Production Editor:	Denise Santoyo
Typesetter:	Siva Math Setters, Chennai, India
Cover Designer:	Michael Dubowe
Production Artist:	Sandra Ng

Contents

Preface

The work of the school administrator is often described as fragmented and unrelenting. Often left unsaid is that the work of the school administrator is lonely.

During the past two years, we have focused our work on an examination of stress and burnout. Our book *Rekindling the Flame: Principals Combating Teacher Burnout* (2000) is a discussion of teacher burnout and the steps principals can take to assist teachers. *Avoiding Burnout: A Principal's Guide to Keeping the Fire Alive* addresses issues related to administrator stress and burnout.

School administrators do not have mirrors to look into to see how they are doing. Because the work of school administration is lonely, they may not have colleagues they can call on to serve as their "mirrors." In this book, we offer school administrators a mirror in the form of voices of school administrators who offer their stories and suggestions about how they handle stress and burnout. Through this approach, administrators can assess themselves in relation to how other administrators manage the complexity and pace of school administration.

We begin with a look at the nature of stress and an assessment of individual stress triggers and response mechanisms. Subsequent chapters outline practical strategies for diminishing stress at home and capitalizing on work stress with effective time-management and interpersonal skills. The last chapter offers suggestions for career renewal and caring for one's personal well-being.

The resources at the end of the book are further tools for self-assessment. Because the professional development and renewal of administrators may be overlooked in the daily work of a school district, we hope that this book will serve as a means of professional reflection and development for school leaders.

ACKNOWLEDGMENTS

The authors gratefully acknowledge Phyllis Hasse for her expertise and skill in preparing this manuscript. We extend appreciation to the many principals who shared their experiences and insights with us. Finally, the contributions of the following reviewers are gratefully acknowledged:

John A. Thacker, Principal
John Motley Morehead High Schools
Eden, NC

Colleen Capper, Professor
Department of Educational Administration
University of Wisconsin–Madison
Madison, WI

Dennis Dunklee, Professor
Graduate School of Education
George Mason University
Fairfax, VA

Kaye L. Peery, Administrator
Springer Municipal Schools
Springer, NM

Barbara L. Brock
Marilyn L. Grady

About the Authors

Barbara L. Brock, Ed.D., is Associate Professor of the Education Department at Creighton University, Omaha, Nebraska. Her research interests include public and nonpublic education, specifically the principalship, leadership succession, and teacher development. She is coauthor, with Marilyn L. Grady, of *Rekindling the Flame: Principals Combating Teacher Burnout*, *From First Year to First Rate: Principals Guiding Beginning Teachers*, and *Principals in Transition: Tips for Surviving Succession*. In addition, she has written for a number of journals, including the *Journal of School Leadership*, *Connections*, *Educational Considerations*, *Clearinghouse*, *Catholic Education: A Journal of Inquiry and Practice*, *Momentum*, and the *Journal of the Mid-Western Research Association*. She has been a teacher and administrator in K-12 schools as well as at the college level. She received her bachelor's degree in art education from Briar Cliff College, Sioux City, Iowa, her master's degree in education with a specialty in school administration from Creighton University, and her doctoral degree in administration, curriculum, and instruction from the University of Nebraska–Lincoln.

Marilyn L. Grady, Ph.D., is Professor of Educational Administration at the University of Nebraska–Lincoln. Her research areas include leadership, the principalship, and superintendent-board relations. She has more than 150 publications to her credit. She is the author or coauthor of 12 books. Her editorial board service includes *Educational Administration Quarterly, The Rural Educator, The Journal of At-Risk Issues,* the *Journal of School Leadership, Advancing Women in Leadership (On-Line Journal),* and the *Journal for a Just and Caring Education.*

She coordinates an annual conference on women in educational leadership that attracts national attendance and is in its 15th year. She has served on the executive board of the National Council of Professors of Educational Administration, the Center for the Study of Small/Rural Schools, and Phi Delta Kappa Chapter 15. She is a member of the American Educational Research Association, the International Academy of Educational Leaders, the National Rural Education Association, the National Council of Professors of Educational Administration, Phi Delta Kappa, and the Horace Mann League. She has been an administrator in K-12 schools as well as at the college and university level. She received her bachelor's degree in history from Saint Mary's College, Notre Dame, Indiana, and her Ph.D. in educational administration with a specialty in leadership from The Ohio State University.

To our children
David and Eric Brock,
Mercedes, Alex, Natasha, Justin, and Elizabeth Grady,
who reside at the center of our world.

CHAPTER ONE

Meeting the Dragon

Getting Acquainted

Stress: When your heart is in one place and your body is in another.

—Anonymous

School principals have profound responsibilities for educating future leaders. A daunting task, it is compounded by dwindling resources, increasing responsibilities, and growing public scrutiny (Amundson, 1993). Stress is a familiar companion.

In ancient times, some cultures feared fire-breathing dragons, while others viewed dragons as good and beneficial. Stress, like the mythological dragon, evokes a similar response. While some people perceive threats lurking around every corner, others anticipate challenges. Perceptions form our reality. Consequently, we create our own dragons.

All human activities, both pleasurable and unpleasurable, generate stress. In fertile school environments, administrators soon encounter the effects of stress. Although a few of them may withdraw, give up, and suffer burnout, others appear to tolerate stress, if not thrive on it.

1

Life without stress is impossible, but the mental and physical anguishes of stress are manageable. In fact, administrators can learn to moderate, even capitalize on, the stress inherent in their work. The purpose of this book is to assist you in finding a level of stress that is invigorating and challenging while diminishing the causes and incidences of negative stress, or distress.

There are no magic answers. Although each of us possesses the power to control stress, how we do that is determined by individual personality and circumstances. The problem of stress reduction is complex, with multiple interconnecting factors.

GOOD AND BAD STRESS: A MATTER OF PERCEPTION

As a definition, we use Selye's (1974): "Stress is the nonspecific response of the body to any demand made upon it" (p. 14). Stress is caused by anything that stimulates us, increases our level of alertness, or is important or significant to us. Even imagined or anticipated changes in events, routine, or health are interpreted as stress.

Typically, we consider stress as something inherently bad for us. But stress is neither good nor bad—it's a part of life. Life without stress would be pretty dull. A certain amount of stress is necessary and productive in our lives. Too much stress may become unpleasant and potentially destructive. The art of stress management is to maintain a level of healthy, enjoyable, and productive stimulation.

Stress evolves in stages. During the first stage, an event (the stressor) affects us. In the second stage, we interpret the event. We may interpret it as stressful yet stimulating, stressful in a negative sense, or not stressful at all. In the third stage, we choose to respond to the stress according to our perceptions. We may employ coping strategies to counteract the stressor. During the fourth stage, the long-range effects of distress appear as symptoms of declining health (Gmelch & Torelli, 1994).

For example, two administrators may approach the same problem with different responses—one suffering the negative stress of fear and anxiety and the other experiencing eustress, or positive stress, in the wake of an exciting challenge.

Two elementary principals are notified of an impending curriculum change. Marsha feels overburdened by too many changes. She is anxious about how to implement the new curriculum and spends sleepless nights worrying about the negative response from teachers. James, however, is delighted to hear of the change. He is excited about the prospect and looks forward to involving the teachers in the changes. In his case, the stress is beneficial and productive.

STRESS TOLERANCE

Chemicals, critical to bodily functioning, carry messages to the brain. When these brain chemicals are functioning properly, we feel in control of life. However, when they malfunction, we feel overwhelmed by the stress of everyday life and enter a state of brain chemical imbalance that we recognize as being overstressed.

The first sign of overstress is usually the inability to obtain a restful sleep. Then pleasureful activities no longer provide pleasure. Life becomes painful and devoid of pleasure. When all of these symptoms coincide—lack of sleep, fatigue, aches, and pains—we feel that life is no longer enjoyable. We feel overwhelmed, out of control, and we cry easily.

Some individuals inherit a low stress tolerance, meaning that the chemical messengers in their brains are not functioning properly. Stress that most people consider normal is overwhelming to them. Not able to cope with the rigor of daily life, they teeter on a fulcrum of perpetual overstress. Physical and mental problems of fatigue, illness, depression, and mood swings become chronic companions (Mind Tools, 2001).

COMMON SOURCES OF STRESS

Sources of stress include our work and lifestyle, the environment in which we live and work, the substances we consume, as well as our overall health. Sources of stress are often unnoticed. Changes in personal relationships, conflicts, overwork, and even extreme weather conditions routinely intensify stress levels. Minor illnesses, allergies, and hormonal changes compound the problem.

Five categories of sources of stress are the following (Mind Tools, 2001):

1. Survival: The body reacts in a survival mode when health or safety is threatened, when we experience pressure, or when we are faced with an unpleasant or challenging event. Adrenaline is released, and the body gears up for either fight or flight.

2. Internally generated stress: We worry about events beyond our control, relationship problems, approaching life in a hurry, being addicted to stress.

3. Environmental stress: It is caused by the noise, crowds, pollution, climate, and general distractions of the environment.

4. Job stress: It is caused by conditions, expectations, and situations at work.

5. Overwork: We try to achieve too much in too little time; we practice ineffective time management

Identifying and understanding factors that trigger our stress enable us to adopt strategies to manage it.

NORMAL STRESS

Daily, short-duration stress is normal. Everyone experiences stressful times. At one end of the continuum is mild stress that we can handle by going home, relaxing, and getting some rest. When stressful periods are of short duration, we cope with the situations and minimize the possibility of long-term damage.

When Normal Stress Becomes Destructive

At the other end of the continuum is distress, stress that is unrelenting and prolonged. Distress may result from an ongoing event or from the ripples of an event that has already occurred. Feelings of discomfort do not disappear when we relax at the end of the day. Instead, we feel out of control and overwhelmed.

Warning signs of stress-related problems include feeling overwhelmed, out of control, extremely sad, constantly fearful, worried, and indecisive. Negative changes in energy level, concentration, sleeping habits, eating habits, and personal relationships may also occur (Brock & Grady, 2000). According to Carruth (1997), emotional exhaustion is the key variable in impending burnout.

If you exhibit signs of distress, you need to heed the warning and find a way to minimize or manage the stress you are experiencing. If you suffer prolonged and unmitigated distress, you are a candidate for serious health problems and professional burnout. An experienced elementary principal reflected, "I realized I had let things go on too long, . . . but by then I was getting so sick."

When Distress Becomes Burnout

Individuals who suffer prolonged and unrelenting stress are candidates for burnout. Psychiatrist Herbert Freudenberger coined the term *burnout* in 1974 to characterize the psychological state of individuals involved in emotionally charged interactions with clients and patients (Brock & Grady, 2000). Maslach (1982) later constructed a broadly accepted model of the phenomenon.

Prior to their studies, burnout clearly existed. In the Old Testament, the prophet Elijah complained of suffering exhaustion and a sense of personal failure. By the 1980s, burnout had become an overused buzzword (Carruth, 1997).

The most widely accepted model of burnout is a three-step process with three elements: emotional exhaustion, depersonalization, and decreased personal accomplishment (Maslach, 1982):

1. Emotional exhaustion results when the emotional demands of the job exceed the emotional resources of the individual. We feel overextended emotionally.

2. Depersonalization is a coping device, apparent in our negative and cynical attitudes toward others.

3. Reduced personal accomplishment refers to our negative self-evaluation of personal accomplishment. A sense of efficacy is lost, self-esteem is threatened.

For school administrators, burnout is increasing. School leaders enter the profession "to make a difference," only to have their hopes and aspirations thwarted by the frustrations of the job. To remain productive when confronted with mounting societal demands, they find both increased accountability and unrelenting change challenges.

THE BURNOUT SYNDROME

Overwork is not the cause of burnout. Burnout occurs when our heart is in one place and our work is in another. The passion dies and we no longer look forward to the work that previously gave us joy. Work is no longer rewarding. We are emotionally, psychologically, or physically exhausted.

Burnout does not occur in one dramatic episode and should not be confused with occasional feelings of unhappiness and discouragement. Rather, it is a progressive, prolonged syndrome that occurs in stages. The feelings become so chronic that individuals are often unaware of the existence of the problem (Brock & Grady, 2000). Burnout victims endure incredible amounts of pain without recognizing their symptoms. They function as if on automatic pilot.

A high school principal described a professional life that was spiraling into burnout: "I worked easily 70 hours a week, sometimes seven days a week. There was the expectation that I had to be there. The anxiety was the worst, . . . feeling like I never knew what was going to happen when I walked in. . . . I was anxious and worried all the time. I started doubting my decisions. . . . I was absorbed, working took over my whole life."

Individuals suffering burnout generally exhibit symptoms in five areas: physical, intellectual, social, emotional, and spiritual (Cedoline, 1982; Farber, 1991; Maslach & Leiter, 1997). The symptoms should not be considered discrete, but multifaceted, with blurred distinctions at their intersections.

Physical. Chronic exhaustion is typical of school administrators suffering burnout. Sleep is no longer refreshing. They feel as exhausted in the morning as they did when they went to bed. The prospect of meeting another person or handling another problem seems overwhelming. Their sleep patterns are disturbed.

Some administrators report sleepless nights, whereas others sleep excessively. One exhausted veteran principal, worried about keeping his position, said, "The amount of sleep on any given night would come to two and one-half to three hours. I would wake up shaking, . . . worried about whether or not I was to have a contract offer the following year." Another said, "If I couldn't sleep, I turned on the TV and watched the old shows, . . . some of those kinds of things to try and stop my thinking, my brain."

Physical symptoms, ailments, weight problems, and minor accidents often occur. Headaches, stomach and intestinal distress, and high blood pressure are common. Some administrators report anxiety, depression, or difficulty concentrating. Sometimes individuals have more accidents—bumping, tripping, or falling. Dismayed by how her health had declined, one elementary principal said, "I started getting sick, . . . gained 50 pounds, . . . my blood pressure soared. I had trouble eating right, couldn't sleep, and suffered migraine headaches."

Intellectual. Individuals under extreme stress have difficulty making decisions. They often delay decisions or vacillate in decision making, unwilling to accept the consequences of their actions. Another elementary principal noted, "My decision making was affected significantly. I started doubting how I was making decisions. I felt I couldn't please anybody." Individuals may feel overwhelmed by information, become mentally disorganized, and find it difficult to remain focused on a task.

Social. Withdrawal from others is a characteristic of individuals suffering burnout. One high school principal said, "When I started getting sick, relationships with family and friends started to deteriorate." A female elementary administrator said, "I talked to my husband a lot about my problems, . . . but I was very careful how much I said because my husband is a peaceful person. To see any human being treated like this, which was in truth abusive, is intolerable to him. So I had to be careful how much I told him. I didn't do any socializing with friends. I was absorbed in my job; it took over my whole life."

Emotional. Individuals initially deny the existence of burnout. When they notice symptoms, they project the blame onto someone or something else. Although outside factors may be instrumental in their burnout, individuals do not recognize the responsibility they have to make changes that will address the issue. One high school principal identified the primary sources of his burnout: "My burnout is caused by the ineffectiveness of my immediate supervisor, . . . also, the high socioeconomic status of the parents. . . . They want to run the school like they do their own companies." However, even when his health suffered, he could not entertain the option of leaving: "Leaving is not in my personality. I can't tell you how many people said I should have left. . . . I was, in essence, being emotionally and professionally abused. . . . I'm amazed at what I will endure because I love the students. . . . I couldn't abandon them. There aren't a lot of people who really know their stuff and can handle this setting."

Individuals become competitive, territorial, and defensive, worrying about their jobs. One elementary principal said, "The worst part was the anxiety. I was anxious all the time. I had the fear of losing my job and not being able to get another." Trust becomes distrust. He reported struggling to mitigate gossip from unknown detractors, and added, "People are saying things about me that aren't true. . . . It's a popularity contest. It doesn't matter if you're incompetent as long as everybody loves you."

Spiritual. Burnout destroys relationships and satisfaction with work. Self-confidence diminishes; spiritual and personal values are shaken. One principal of a parochial school sought relief through religion: "I prayed tons . . . candles, music, and the whole nine yards, . . . also the breathing. The thing that seemed to help the most was the praying. I went on an all-day retreat . . . and had a spiritual mentor. I tried to use self-affirmation and it didn't work. I had allowed my supervisor to undermine my self-esteem."

Who's at Risk?

You may be at risk of burnout if you can identify yourself on this list (Mind Tools, 2001):

- You find it hard, or impossible, to say no to additional responsibilities or commitments.

- You have been working under pressure for a long period of time.
- You have been trying to achieve too much for a long period of time.
- You feel more comfortable doing it yourself, and find it difficult to delegate.
- You have been the source of emotional support for others for too long.

Make no mistake—burnout is a detriment to your health as well as your career and should be taken seriously. The best prevention is to recognize the early warning signs of prolonged stress and take corrective action. Early warning signs include

- Feelings of mental and physical exhaustion
- Feeling out of control, overwhelmed
- An increase in negative thinking
- Increased isolation from family, friends, and colleagues
- A sense of declining productivity or lack of accomplishment
- Dreading going to work in the morning

If you are in danger of burnout, it is critical to examine the sources of your discomfort and adopt corrective strategies. The stress management techniques discussed in this book are presented not as a cure but as a preventative measure to avoid burnout.

There is no quick fix for someone suffering from burnout. If you are already experiencing burnout or feel that life and work have lost their pleasure, medical and psychological assistance may be necessary. Talk with someone who has the professional skills to assist you.

Avoiding Depression

Despite efforts to avoid it, educational leaders are not exempt from depression. In fact, the stress imposed by hectic schedules and unresolved burnout can be contributors. Depression is signaled by feelings of distress that do not go away. Life seems devoid of joy.

More than 10 million people in the United States may suffer from depression. This serious and treatable problem often goes undiagnosed and untreated because we do not recognize the symptoms and fail to seek appropriate help (Toy, 1998).

As with any potential illness, you should not undertake self-diagnosis. Rather, you should report your symptoms to an appropriate health care professional.

Symptoms of depression can include (Toy, 1998):

- A loss of interest or pleasure in something previously enjoyed
- Difficulty concentrating or remembering
- Physical pain (not attributed to a known injury or illness)
- Sleep disturbances
- Changes in appetite
- Unusual irritability
- Loss of self-esteem or indifference
- Prolonged feelings of sadness
- Frequent crying spells

Burnout and Rustout

There is a difference between administrators who burn out and those who rust out. Administrators at risk of burnout are hard workers with a passionate commitment to their jobs. They became administrators because they believed they could make schools better for students. Often their work becomes the focus of their lives and their identities. The factor that creates a risk for burnout is the same factor that makes them good administrators—their dedication to their work. When they are not rewarded or recognized, though, disillusionment can lead to burnout.

The rustouts initially entered school administration to (a) escape the classroom or (b) advance on the pay scale. In either case, they did not have a burning desire to become a school administrator. Although some of these administrators are competent (a few even excellent school leaders), most of them lack the zeal to be candidates for burnout.

These rustouts demonstrate from the outset that administration is not their ideal career choice. However, returning to classroom teaching may be unwelcome and perceived as an embarrassing step backwards. Financial circumstances force others to remain, albeit unhappy, in administrative positions.

Although the amount of stress inherent in the work of a school principal is often unchangeable, they can change how they respond to stress. They have the power to control stress. Administrators can reduce the negative aspects of stress and avoid the risk of burnout, even improve their performance, by learning how to manage stress and channel it in positive directions. If they don't do this, relentless stress can lead to serious medical problems and depression.

SUMMARY

Stress is neither good nor bad—it's a part of life. Life without stress would be pretty dull. Sources of stress include our work and lifestyle, the environment in which we live and work, the substances we consume, as well as our overall health. Identifying and understanding factors that trigger our stress enable us to adopt strategies to manage it. In the next chapter, we identify stress triggers.

CHAPTER TWO

Provoking the Dragon

Stress Triggers

The longest journey of any person is the journey inward.

—Dag Hammarskjöld

Stress is a function of personality characteristics combined with personal and workplace issues. Although one factor may dominate, the precise cause of stress usually occurs at their intersection. An examination of the contributions of personality, personal issues, and workplace factors to stress is helpful.

INTERNALLY GENERATED STRESS

Some individuals possess personalities that increase their proclivity to stress and burnout. Factors such as self-concept, perfectionism, locus of control, and personality type influence stress.

Self-Concept

Self-concept is a predictor of burnout. An individual with low self-esteem is more likely to be overwhelmed by the emotional pressures of an administrator's work. People and pressures consume and emotionally exhaust them. Unable to cope with mounting difficulties and obstacles, their low self-evaluation is confirmed.

Empathic self-esteem, or our perceptions of how others think of us, is also a predictor of burnout. School administrators who try to live up to others' expectations and standards become emotionally exhausted and prone to burnout. One elementary principal described lessons she learned during her first year:

> I always said that if I become an administrator, I would not have teachers overburdened with supervising the halls, cafeteria, and playground. So, I did all of that for them. I also wanted everybody to like me. I couldn't understand how I could do all of these things, and there was always a teacher who was never satisfied. I was really upset by that. I also took on the personal problems of the staff. At the beginning, I didn't see a problem because I wanted to be compassionate. I wanted teachers to bring their personal problems to me. I gave advice, went to their homes, took them to dinner . . . and then the problems began. Word spread. Teachers were calling me at home. I no longer had time for my own family. I soon learned some important lessons: not everyone would like me or agree with my decisions, and not all of the problems belonged to me.

Perfectionism

Perfectionists feel that they need do everything perfectly. They are paralyzed by a fear of not performing well enough or, even worse, failing at something. They assign enormous power to the fear of imperfection. As a result, they overwork. They cannot delegate because they believe no one can do the job as well as they can. They isolate themselves to avoid disclosing any imperfections. Meanwhile, personal production lags due to indecision, missed deadlines, and micromanaging. Too focused on minutiae, their perfectionism becomes career limiting (Gallagher, 2000).

Locus of Control

Individuals with an external locus of control perceive the world as happening to them. They feel that they have little control over what happens to them. As one administrator explained, "We are at the mercy of people who know nothing about what we do. They have complete control over whether or not we can or cannot do our jobs or whether or not we will or will not have a job." Individuals with an external locus of control tend to blame others for their lives. Describing how his burnout was caused, one elementary administrator said, "I was a victim of my supervisor." This feeling of being out of control and helpless increases feelings of stress.

Individuals with an internal locus of control have an "I can" attitude. They feel that they are in charge of the circumstances of their lives. Subsequently, they suffer less stress and are less likely to suffer burnout (Brady, 1989; Lennon, 1992). One veteran high school principal explained, "I look at conflicts and problems as challenges for me to solve. I also decide who owns the problem; not all the problems are mine. Also, not everyone is going to like me or my decisions . . . and that's OK."

Personality Type

Another predictor of burnout is personality type. Are you always in a hurry, impatient, competitive, with high expectations for yourself? Then you may be a type A person. People with this personality type are compulsive overachievers, who set unrealistic expectations for themselves and subsequently assume heavy workloads. They enjoy delaying work until the last minute, saying, "I work better under pressure." However, their enjoyment of deferred deadlines creates extra stress for colleagues. Type A administrators are susceptible to burnout themselves and tend to increase the likelihood of burnout for people who work for them (Chaney & Forbes, 1989; Nagy, 1983; Ravicz, 1997).

Individuals with type B personalities are more relaxed and mellow in their approach. A self-described type B principal, who weathered 26 years of school administration, explained, "I see no reason to become upset about things I can't change. However, this is something that I had to learn and practice."

THE CONTRIBUTIONS
OF GENDER TO STRESS

When women care for their children, despite demanding careers, it's expected; when men do the same, they are exalted as great fathers.

—Barbara Brock

The role of gender in professional burnout continues to be debated. Marriage, pregnancy, childbirth, and child care do bring additional responsibilities to women with administrative careers. Stress may occur, not specifically to either role, but due to the incompatibility of the roles (Aneshensel & Pearlin, 1987).

Unlike their male counterparts, who often assign child care to their spouses, the married career woman remains the primary caretaker of the children. Although societal norms are changing, many women continue to experience stress due to the demands of work mingled with the strain of managing household tasks and child care. The husband's perception of his parental role is an important factor. If both partners perceive him to be an "equal partner" in caring for the children, the woman will experience less stress. If the father perceives himself to be a "helper" in the process, then the responsibility rests clearly with the mother, increasing her chances for conflict and stress. Regardless of the helpfulness of the spouse, when a woman's perceptions of her role as wife and mother conflict with those of her role as a school administrator, she suffers guilt and stress (Aneshensel & Pearlin, 1987). As one female administrator pointed out, "The condition of the house and how well the kids are cared for still reflects on the wife."

One female administrator reflected on the dual role she held when her children were young:

Coming home from work was like going to a second job. To this day, I still despise cooking. When it was just my husband and me, I didn't mind it. But once the kids got here, I really started to hate cooking. It would be so late by the time the kitchen was cleaned up and the kids were in bed; it was 11:00 before I had time to myself. I just wanted to be left alone. That was the only time I had for myself, my quiet time.

Another principal, who described her husband as a "good helper," expressed frustration: "I was infuriated when my husband sat watching TV with his feet on the coffee table and inquired what was for dinner!"

Women are sometimes frustrated by their spouse's perception of his job as the number one priority. One elementary administrator said, "My job was considered a second priority to him. He always said, 'If I get such and such a position, we're moving.' He had little regard for the impact of a move on my career goals." Although moves are issues for both genders, often it is the woman's career that is geographically defined by her spouse's career.

Some female administrators describe bringing a spouse to school-related events as stressful. One principal said, "I know my spouse is going only because he feels he has to. I feel guilty and worried about his not having a good time. . . . It's stressful for me."

The sparsity of women in school administration results in a lack of role models and subsequent supportive professional relationships. As women define themselves in terms of human relationships, the lack of a professional support system produces stress (Gilligan, 1982).

Perfectionism is an additional problem for women because they tie self-image and self-worth to how others perceive them, and they fear being wrong or inadequate (Gallagher, 2000). One high school principal described her problem with perfectionism:

> If I hadn't given up that rigid pace, doing everything myself and acting as though I was the only one who could do it right, I wouldn't have made it. And I still feel that way to a degree. If there are some things that I want done to perfection, then I still want to do them myself.

Some women feel that they need to outperform their male counterparts to be successful. This perception causes women to drive themselves often at the expense of their health (Dillihunt, 1986). In addition, some researchers have found that women feel powerless and less influential than men in their working situations and experience more burnout than men (Leitner, Clark, & Durup, 1994, as cited in Carruth, 1997).

Looking at the Male Perspective

The dual roles of administrator and homemaker contribute to stress for males as well as females. Time-honored societal expectations for men to provide financially for the family and women to care for home and children have changed. Many women are major contributors to family finances and often consider their jobs equal to, if not more important than, their spouses.

With the male model of past generations no longer relevant, men struggle to find and adapt to new roles and emergent stress. A 50-year-old high school principal commented, "My wife was home caring for our children. I can't imagine the difficulties of managing two careers and a family." However, for many men, two-career families are the reality, one that requires new solutions for child care, housekeeping, shopping, and meal preparation. No longer the sole breadwinners, men are expected to be active participants in child rearing and domestic duties. The added responsibilities, however, have enabled fathers to participate in raising their children, which for many men has become a source of great satisfaction.

ETHNICITY AND STRESS

Our ethnic origin may contribute to tensions at work. Administrators belonging to a minority group may find themselves resented because they were selected for the job. They are often singled out for scrutiny. Colleagues and parents question their competence and skills. Parents watch for signs of racism. One African American principal recalled,

When I was a principal in a predominately black inner-city school, white parents complained that I punished their children too harshly for racial slurs, saying that I probably wouldn't have suspended a black child. When I moved to a primarily white school, I encountered a group of parents who didn't respect my authority. In their opinion, I was an African American and didn't understand conditions or problems that affected Caucasian families. Other parents expressed the opinion that black principals should be placed in predominately black schools and white principals in white schools. Personally, I had difficulty treating some of these parents with respect when I knew how they felt about people of color. However, I was careful to maintain district policies and guidelines when dealing with them.

Administrators who are members of minority groups are frequently sought for committee service, which increases their workload. Black females encounter another set of problems. If they have competed with black males for an administrative position, they may be accused by their peers of contributing to society's denigration of black males. Unmarried female administrators seeking to marry a black male with a similar professional background and income will find a small pool of eligible applicants. Married women, black and white, who achieve incomes higher than their spouses sometimes generate marital tension (Pigford & Tonnsen, 1993).

Personal Issues

Personal circumstances may contribute to feelings of stress at work. When suffering job-related stress, we ordinarily seek a cause within the workplace. However, personal problems may exacerbate an already stressful work environment (Huberman, 1993; Kijai & Totten, 1995). Issues such as family illness or death, marital or relationship problems, difficulties with children, chemical dependence, and financial problems evoke strong emotions that are difficult to leave at home and may interfere with job performance.

Personal issues to consider include

- Raising children and running a home while working full time (if you are a single parent, the burden increases)
- Caring for aging parents
- Dealing with personal or a family member's illness
- Dealing with a chemically dependent family member
- Extreme behavior problems with a child
- Birth or adoption of a child
- Marital problems
- Newly married
- Financial problems

- Recent death in the family
- Moving to a different home
- Remodeling a home
- Child leaving home

These are just a few of the personal issues that may add a layer of stress to an already stressful job. Any change in personal circumstances, whether positive or negative, adds a layer of stress. Whenever circumstances at home create heavy physical and emotional burdens in addition to job responsibilities, the accumulation of factors increases stress and the risk for burnout. Although we may not be able to or want to lessen our responsibilities, it is important to identify what is creating stress and find a way to lessen the negative impacts of the stress.

WORKPLACE FACTORS

Some occupational and workplace stressors are universal to all school administrators. The categories identified by Gmelch & Torelli (1994) define the types of situations that administrators commonly find stressful:

- Role: the administrator's perception of his or her role in the school (based on personal beliefs and attitudes)
- Task: caused by daily activities (such as phone calls, meetings, reports, interruptions, and evening school functions)
- Boundary spanning: stress caused by external issues (such as gaining public support)
- Conflict: caused by handling conflicts between individuals and between individuals and the school

Role-Based Stress

Role-based stress occurs when administrators are given competing roles or the administrator's role is not clearly defined in terms of behavior or role expectations. When administrators are given two or more incompatible directives, they experience stress. One elementary administrator gave this example:

Parents are clamoring for increased computer education for the students. The board of education agrees with them and has directed me to make it happen. The computer lab is lacking and needs an update. However, I'm not allowed a budget increase to acquire additional computers and software. This is a no-win situation.

Workplace conditions, such as a poor facility and lack of resources, conflict with the high-performance expectations placed on the administrator. Sometimes responsibilities and expectations are ambiguous. One elementary principal reported this situation: "My supervisor is displeased because he's receiving parent complaints about me. I've asked him to share the complaints and tell me if and how he would like me to change my behavior. He refuses to discuss it. . . . He just tells me to figure it out and take care of it."

School district policies and procedures and supervisory structure contribute to role-based conflict. A lack of clarity regarding expectations and contradictory roles contribute to interpersonal conflict, creating another layer of stress. Role conflict and role ambiguity are prominent factors in administrative stress and burnout (Gmelch & Torelli, 1994).

Tasks

School administrators are prepared to work for long hours. Their day often begins with a phone call before they leave home and continues with a parent waiting for them in the parking lot. All day long, interruptions plague them as they race the clock to meet deadlines. They place a high value on hard work, honesty, integrity, and effective teaching (Whan & Thomas, 1996). Their stress levels rise when the teachers they supervise exhibit values contrary to theirs. Teachers' lack of dedication, professionalism, work ethic, and honesty causes additional stress for administrators. A study by Whan & Thomas (1996) identified the following teacher behaviors as producing stress for principals:

- Sitting at their desk rather than moving around the classroom
- Being late for supervision responsibilities
- Inadequate lesson preparation

- Using removal from class or a trip to the principal as punishment
- Blaming others for problems
- Discourteous treatment of others
- Being late with administrative chores
- Being negative, unsupportive, or uncooperative
- Complaining about work issues

Inadequate performance of members of the office staff compounds the stress (Whan & Thomas, 1996). Other stressful administrative tasks (Whan & Thomas, 1996) include

- Finding substitutes for teacher absences
- Staff meetings, particularly when a controversial issue is raised or expected
- Working with parent groups, especially when parents are uncooperative
- Implementing government mandates or policies
- Problems with shortages, deliveries, and equipment
- School break-ins, theft, and vandalism
- Work overload
- Time constraints
- Extracurricular duties (student activities outside of school hours)
- Meetings outside of school hours
- Working in isolation
- Lack of resources for a task
- Lack of appreciation
- Lack of control in decisions

Boundary Spanning

The high public visibility of an administrator's job under-scores it with stress. Every action and decision is subject to scrutiny, suspicion, and misunderstanding. Criticism of public schools and demands for change are increasing. Citizen activism for school change is becoming prevalent. Changing educational practices or procedures that require community support demand careful planning. When parent organizations seek power, demand immediate or impossible changes, or are generally disagreeable, the situation is explosive. The threat of potential professional damage from a concerted attack by parent lobbyists is intimidating (Whan & Thomas, 1996).

Conflict

Conflict is a familiar companion in the world of school administration: "I soon realized that not everyone would be happy with my decisions." Administrators cannot expect to please all the parents all the time. Nevertheless, encounters with angry or displeased parents are stressful. The possibilities of continued complaints, gossip, or a damaged reputation are constant aspects of school administration (Whan & Thomas, 1996).

Conflict with difficult or discontented personnel is tedious. Administrators must intercede to resolve conflicts between staff members, between staff members and parents, and between staff members and students (Whan & Thomas, 1996). One high school principal commented on her role as mediator: "I felt like there was a sign over my office door that read, 'Conflicts welcome, come one, come all.'"

Sometimes conflict is caused by an administrator's management style. Those who rely on the power of their position stimulate conflict. Use of position power tends to cause more conflict and more stress for the administrator.

Principals who manage through personal power usually interact well with people and generate less conflict. They enjoy strong social support and subsequently experience less stress and less burnout (Carruth, 1997).

Stress is also precipitated by student misbehavior. Principals in schools where students have severe behavior problems feel overburdened and frustrated, whereas other principals report that stress from adult conflicts exceeds student behavior problems (Whan & Thomas, 1996). Other principals report that student apathy is of greater concern than overt conflict.

Administrators describe stressful work settings as ones in which

- Expectations are unclear
- Criterion for measuring success is absent

- Job security is uncertain
- Demands are unrealistic and unreasonable
- Financial problems exist
- The staff is new or inexperienced
- Personal problems exist
- Security/safety is an issue
- Citizen activism for radical changes is present

As the number of organizational stress factors increases, so too does the administrator's personal stress level. Understanding issues that are the source of stress at work allows them to confront those issues and make changes.

Societal Norms

Compounding the role of the administrator is a culture that supports, even prizes, workaholism. Working long hours is often touted as the way to succeed. An addictive process, work becomes central to the workaholic's life. They are energized by work and find it difficult to relax on weekends. The stress they experience and generate, however, is harmful to their health and relationships (Schaef & Fassel, 1990).

SUMMARY

Stress is a function of personality characteristics combined with personal and workplace issues. Factors such as self-concept, perfectionism, locus of control, and personality type influence stress. Gender issues and ethnic origin may also contribute to stress. Personal problems may exacerbate an already stressful work environment. In the next chapter, we identify responses to stress and emphasize the importance of identifying goals and a vision of success.

CHAPTER THREE

Confronting the Dragon Within

Mental Restructuring

Sometimes . . . I would welcome a calamity of nature . . . erasing all that I have except the opportunity to begin again.

—Ric Masten (*The Survivors*, 1979)

Administrators search for ways to eliminate or cope with stress. Faced with stressful situations, they may make destructive choices, using sugar, caffeine, alcohol, and tobacco to temporarily restore equilibrium. See Resource A for a listing of destructive and positive responses to stress.

The problem with using substances as energy or pleasure boosters is that their effect is temporary and their habitual use creates other problems. Some individuals maintain a constant supply of one or more of these substances in their bodies. Margaret, for example, consumes sweet rolls and coffee in the morning and switches to cola and candy later in the day. Terry looks forward to relaxing over chips and dip, several beers, and cigars after work each day. Janice relies on medications to help her sleep at night and stay awake during the day. Although seemingly harmless substances, daily indulgence may create long-term health problems. Meanwhile, the issues that caused their stress are not addressed.

Other individuals use bingeing as a stress reliever. They generally maintain healthful diets. However, when their stress builds to an intolerable level, they indulge in binge eating or drinking until they feel a sense of relief. The resulting weight gain, guilt, or mounting credit card bills further accentuate their stress.

Destructive responses to stress not only compound the underlying problem but become habits that generate a new set of problems. A retired elementary principal reflected,

> I knew that I would never let myself get to a point where I needed medications or psychological care because of a job. I was determined never to get to a point where I had to take pills to get to sleep and pills to wake up.

Stress can be averted or managed through strategies such as identifying goals, adjusting an attitude, changing perspectives, or removing stressful circumstances. Although it is common to blame other people and situations, the source of stress may be self-imposed. Stress may originate from attitudes, perspectives, and ill-suited career or life choices. Rather than seeking external changes, it is more productive to alter personal attitudes, perspectives, and behaviors.

When you are out of touch with who you are and what you want, the result may be an unhappy career or life choice. Mounting divorce rates, as well as the number of school administrators who regret leaving their former positions, are examples of unhappy choices.

Self-knowledge and goals are critical to making significant career or life choices. These decisions require you to clarify personal values, beliefs, goals, and attitudes and know who you are and what you want. Satisfaction and happiness are the result of achieving goals that are compatible with your personal values and beliefs.

PLANNING FOR LIFE'S JOURNEY

Instead of thinking about where you are, think about where you want to be. It takes 20 years of hard work to become an overnight success.

—Diana Rankin

Tom had been a principal for five years. Although he worked hard, he found little satisfaction in his job. He was anxious, worried, and felt like a failure most of the time. The fact that his parents had both been successful administrators in the same school district made his failures particularly embarrassing. For the first time in his life, he questioned his choice of careers and wondered how he ended up in this situation.

Wandering through life without a plan can be disastrous. Although some individuals stumble into happy careers and relationships, most individuals do not. Unhappy careers and miserable relationships stem from a failure to establish and fulfill personal goals. Individuals such as Tom may think they are following personal goals, when, in fact, they are striving to fulfill goals that their parents, partners, or associates hold for them. The outcome is a life devoid of satisfaction and happiness.

Life's Journey

Enjoy today; this is not a dress rehearsal.

—Anonymous

The length of time between birth and death, called the dash by one unknown author, is the substance of a life. The dash represents actions and relationships, how we lived and loved. Given the finite period of our life, it is important to decide how to spend it.

Maps provide directions toward a destination. Although the journey may involve detours, wrong turns, even getting lost, without the map we would never reach the goal. Most people would not attempt a trip in unfamiliar territory without a map.

However, many people wander through life without a predetermined goal and a road map for their life's journey. Other people mistakenly follow someone else's goals or goals that others have set for them. Sometimes people begin careers with goals but neglect to periodically review and revise the goals in view of new circumstances. Although a few people may wander into a fulfilling career, most do not. Wanderers usually find themselves unhappy, disillusioned, unfulfilled, or burned out, and wondering, "What happened?"

Each life has a unique destination and road map that is revealed only through self-examination and reflection. Modeling and feedback from others may help, but there are no preordained maps and nobody else can provide directions.

"Who am I? What do I want to do with my life? What do I value? What am I capable of doing? What are my strengths? What are my weaknesses? What do I want to achieve in my lifetime? How do I want to be remembered?"

The answers to these questions provide the basis for personal goals. Having a plan based on these goals provides a framework and perspective that shapes choices and decisions. Equally important is making certain that the goals are yours and not those prescribed for you by someone else (Chance & Grady, 1990, 1991; Grady & LeSourd, 1989/1990; LeSourd, & Grady, 1989/1990, 1991; LeSourd, Tracz, & Grady, 1992).

CHARTING A COURSE

Those who lose dreaming are lost.

—Australian Aborigine proverb

Picture the life you want and write down your goals to achieve that life. A personal goal statement should be a growing document that reflects your personal visions and values with criteria for measuring achievements.

Having a direction enables you to behave in ways that align you with that direction. As circumstances change, you can review and revise your plans accordingly.

After determining your goals, assign priorities. Be sure that the goals reflect your personal image of your desired circumstances in life. As those circumstances change, review and adjust the goals.

Action Plans

Often personal goal statements lie buried in a bottom desk drawer. To be attained, goals need to be translated into plans for specific action. Breaking each goal into smaller increments and attaching specific actions to each increment make it more likely that you will achieve the goal.

First, decide what actions and behaviors will allow you to achieve the goal. For each long-term goal, set incremental objectives, such as 6 months, 1 year, 5 years, 10 years, and 20 years. To be most effective, goals should be

- Positively stated
- Precise, including dates, times, and amounts
- Prioritized
- Written down
- Divided into small, incremental steps
- Based on personal performance (not subject to conditions beyond your control)
- Measurable
- Realistic
- Challenging but attainable

Goals are achieved through purposeful daily actions. Some people review their goals and plans at the start of each day. Others reflect in the evening and plan for the following day. Whatever the process, success requires perseverance with a focus on the long-term goal.

As you mature and your experience increases, you may need to revise your goals. Sometimes a goal is no longer needed or desirable. Surprisingly, letting go of a long-held goal, especially if it was influenced by parents or significant others, is difficult. Sometimes people remain in careers that no longer interest them but hesitate to change their career goals. A disheartened high school administrator explained, "I always wanted to be a teacher and principal. I took pride in my profession. But now, I've lost my zeal. I want to do something else, but I'll feel like a failure if I leave the profession. What will my family and friends think?"

Developing an Educational Philosophy

Winners can tell you where they are going, what they plan to do along the way, and who will be sharing the adventure with them.

—Denis Waitley

A clear educational philosophy is essential for educators. Those who aspire to educational leadership need a sense of what they value and a personal vision to guide their journey (Sergiovanni, 1995). Blumberg and Greenfield (cited in Sergiovanni, 1980) concluded that successful school leaders are highly goal oriented and have a keen sense of goal clarity.

Awareness of our core values and beliefs is a prerequisite to making good decisions, handling criticism, and dealing with job frustrations. Equally important is selecting employment in a school district that shares similar values. Conflicting vision and values between principal and school district create stress and frustration that lead to burnout. Selecting employment situations that support our educational philosophy is critical to job satisfaction and success.

Modifying Personality Traits

Everyone thinks of changing the world, but no one thinks of changing himself.

—Leo Tolstoy

Some individuals have lofty goals but engage in behaviors that thwart their progress. Self-defeating personality traits, attitudes, perspectives, and behaviors are major impediments. Personality traits related to locus of control, and perfection may pose obstacles (Brady, 1989; Lennon, 1992).

Changing Locus of Control

People are always blaming their circumstances. I don't believe in circumstances. People who get on in this world are the people who

get up and look for the circumstances they want, and if they can't
find them, make them.

—George Bernard Shaw

Interviews with two successful elementary principals revealed their personality traits, attitudes, perspectives, and behaviors. Consider George's story:

I burned out because I had no support from my superintendent. In fact, he actually created stress for me. He was so
incompetent that he created stress. Parents wanted to run
the school, so I had innate stress right there. I was the only
administrator in the building, and I didn't have enough help. I
did everything myself, worked 70 hours a week. I found out
from other people that the supervisor was furious about
things I did, but he never told me directly.

According to George, the circumstances at his school were out of his control. Although some of the circumstances may have been beyond his control, some of his victimlike stance contributed to his burnout.

James, however, perceived the problems as within his power to change.

I moved from a small school with an easygoing group of fairly
noninvolved parents to a school with 500 students and
parents who were very involved. I was used to doing things
on my own, so this was a shock. The first PTA meeting was
standing room only. These parents were demanding, wanted
to run the building, make room assignments, take kids out of
class at will. I had a problem. I wanted to retain their involve-
ment, but I couldn't allow them to make administrative decisions. Both of us needed to change attitudes and make some
concessions to make this work. I had several meetings with
parents, and while it was difficult at times, we worked it out.

Your locus of control can change by refocusing your attitudes. If you know that you tend to feel controlled by outside
circumstances, consciously try to adopt an "I can" attitude.

When situations begin to feel out of control, distance yourself mentally, rethink the issues that appear to be out of your control, and identify aspects that you can control. Take charge of the circumstances that you can change.

Successful leaders have an internal locus of control. Research indicates that strong leaders do not make premature judgments on what they can or cannot do. Instead of succumbing to external constraints, they view them as challenges to be mastered. External power is viewed as something to be harnessed and used for the good of the school (Blumberg & Greenfield, 1980, as cited in Sergiovanni, 1995). The attitude of strong leaders is "I can do it regardless of . . ." rather than "I can't because of . . ."

GETTING RID OF PERFECTIONISM

Oysters never make mistakes.

—Anonymous

Although oysters never make mistakes, they rarely accomplish much, other than an occasional pearl. School leaders who are perfectionists may limit themselves to a single tiny pearl rather than cultivating a strand of pearls.

Perfectionists are stifled by a fear of mistakes. They spend hours perfecting work that does not warrant the time or attention. By focusing on minutiae, their long-term goals and plans are often neglected. Although overworked, perfectionists seldom delegate tasks, fearing that others may not be as capable as they are. One principal described her struggle:

In my early years of administration, I did everything myself. I spent hours poring over paperwork, . . . and took a lot of it home. I didn't delegate because I was afraid they wouldn't do it as well as I did. I worried about mistakes, especially with things that went to the district. Eventually, I became so overworked that I knew I had to entrust others with some of the tasks. However, I still struggle with this to a degree. . . . If there are things that I want done to perfection, then I have to do them myself.

If you're a perfectionist, acknowledge it and give yourself permission to make a mistake. Try to determine the basis of your perfection so you can deal with it (Gallagher, 2000). Remind yourself that perfection is impossible. Tape a reminder to your desk—ask a friend or coworker to remind you. When you find yourself lingering over a task, ask yourself, "How important is this task in terms of personal or professional goals?" "How much time does it deserve?" Concentrate on creating a strand of pearls rather than one perfect pearl.

A high school principal explained,

> I expect to do things at a pretty high level. Sometimes I make sure that every *i* is dotted and *t* is crossed, . . . but sometimes I just get it done. I can live with myself turning in something that isn't perfect because I've learned to do that. As time becomes shorter for each task, I've learned how to walk away.

SLOWING THE PACE

Life is too important to be taken seriously.

—Anonymous

Mark is always in a hurry and impatient. He has a type A personality. Even the minor inconveniences of daily life, such as lines, traffic, and mechanical failures, cause him extreme aggravation and anger. He has high expectations for himself as well as the people who work with him. A hard worker, he spends long hours at the office, takes work home, and expects the same hours and dedication from everyone else. Unfortunately, Mark's chances for success are being undermined by his stress level, which produces a tension-filled climate at work, posing a threat of burnout for everyone who works there.

It's common for administrators to exhibit type A behaviors. These behaviors, however, do not need to overtake and determine their personality. They can change their attitudes and moderate their behaviors.

When Mark recognizes that his hurried and impatient behavior causes stress, he can make a conscious effort to change his behavior. For example, while driving to work, he can choose to let stress dominate him or he can acknowledge that he cannot change the pace of traffic and, instead, use the time to relax, listen to music, or plan his day. When he becomes frustrated with one aspect of work, his frustrations need not spill over to the next task or person. He can choose to take a moment to relax and compose himself. Serenity arrives with acceptance of the fact that some things cannot be changed. Some issues do not deserve our attention. Focus should be on important issues.

Identifying, acknowledging, and explaining behaviors may help defuse stress. As one female high school principal explained,

> My people would say that I'm a type A personality, not only for myself but my expectations for others too. If I ask you for something, I would like it within 24 hours. Please don't keep me hanging, because too many other things have come across my desk, and I don't want to have to remember that you didn't get that to me. That's the biggest challenge my leadership team deals with: they have things to take care of in their jobs and then to get additional requests from me.

Learning to do one thing at a time and enjoying the pleasure of each moment may be difficult for some individuals. However, these abilities increase creativity and productivity while decreasing workplace stress. Taking life at a slower pace requires practice, but the rewards include greater enjoyment and better health.

Helpful strategies include

- Ignoring the unimportant
- Assigning less importance to events
- Distancing yourself from the problem
- Controlling emotions
- Applying sound problem-solving strategies
- Allowing others to help

ADJUSTING THE LENS

As a man thinks, so he is.

—Proverbs 23:7

How we perceive the world is based on innate traits combined with years of experience. Individuals can control their lives and influence their circumstances by how they respond to events. The first step, however, is awareness and acknowledgment of our attitudes, perspectives, and behaviors. In 1897, the philosopher William James wrote, "The greatest discovery of my generation is that human beings, by changing the inner attitudes of their minds, can change the outer aspects of their lives."

Successful school leaders have a high tolerance for stress. They are able to consider and analyze problems objectively, without being overwhelmed by them (Blumberg & Greenfield, 1980, as cited in Seriogiovanni, 1995). Their actions are based on facts rather than emotions. Some individuals naturally tolerate stress better than others, but most school leaders learn it from years of practice.

Assigning Power

The amount of stress produced by an event is proportional to the importance assigned to the event. By assigning less power to an event, less stress is produced. If a school leader perceives an event as important or urgent, stress will result. The stress will intensify if the leader feels inadequate to accomplish a task. If an event is perceived as unimportant, little or no stress results. In other words, you have the power to control your stress by controlling the power you assign to events.

One elementary principal described how she learned to assign less power to events:

When I was a new principal, I was keenly aware that I was one of a handful of women of color in the district. I knew I was being scrutinized. I felt that I had to prove myself. I worried and labored over everything that I turned in to the district office, afraid that I would make errors and look incompetent. As time went by, I felt accepted and less stressful about making errors. I stopped worrying about the district reports.

DISCARDING TRIVIAL STRESSORS

Frequently, time is wasted by fretting over insignificant issues. Worrying and being upset about small issues diverts attention from important issues. Concentrate, instead, on important issues.

The *injured party syndrome* is one example of misdirected energy. Some people harbor injustices for years. They are consumed with anger and bitterness from some wrong they feel was inflicted on them. People blame everyone from parents, lovers, and ex-spouses to former teachers, employers, and colleagues. Destructive moods, feelings of self-worth, and nonproductive responses are intertwined with feelings toward this person or event.

The solution is simple. Grow up. Get over it. Move on. Liberate yourself from being controlled by persons or events.

PUTTING WORRIES IN PERSPECTIVE

It's all right to have butterflies in your stomach. Just get them to fly in formation.

—Rob Gilbert

Most of us can identify with Mark Twain, who said, "My life has been a series of endless crises, most of which never happened." Worrying about future events is a common yet futile practice. However, we can learn to dissipate stress by looking at problems from a mental distance, as though they belonged to somebody else. Perspectives change when we consider

- Why is this important to me?
- How important is this problem?
- Will anybody remember this problem in a week, month, or year?
- What's the worst possible thing that can happen?
- How likely is it to happen?
- How long will this situation last?
- What can I do to resolve the problem?

Restructuring Versus Worrying

I used to fret and worry when people were upset. It took me a long time to learn that it's impossible to make everyone happy. Now I approach conflicts as challenging problems for

me to solve rather than personal criticisms. I remind myself
that the other person owns the problem. When I learn that
a parent is upset, I don't wait for them to explode; I take the
initiative and contact them to see if I can be of assistance in
solving their problem.

The words of an elementary principal describe how she used
cognitive restructuring to deal with conflict. She transferred
ownership of the conflict from herself to the parent. The problem
became one she could solve rather than an emotional issue.

Cognitive restructuring is useful for controlling emotional
responses. The process involves thinking about an event and decid-
ing how to respond to it. Subsequent actions and feelings are influenced by the thought process (Young, 1998). Consider the mental
steps that Janice, a high school principal, takes in this scenario:

Janice dreads the meeting with Mrs. Jones this afternoon, the
fourth one in the last 6 weeks. Mrs. Jones is a chronic com-
plainer and gossiper. This time she alleges (and has spread the
story throughout the community) that Mr. Smith was verbally offensive and used crude language when disciplining
her daughter. According to several witnesses, the allegations
are totally unfounded.

Janice is furious and is tempted to be verbally offensive in
return. Instead, she takes time before the meeting to breathe
deeply and compose herself. She gathers all the facts surround-
ing the incident and reminds herself that this is not a personal
issue, but a difference in opinion. Mrs. Jones deserves courtesy
and respectful treatment. She tells herself that she will not
be drawn into a verbal confrontation. Instead, she will listen
carefully, state the facts, and resolve the issue.

She writes the steps for conflict resolution on her notepad
as a reminder of how she will organize the meeting. She
writes down Mrs. Jones's complaint to help keep the conversation focused on the immediate problem.

Janice reminds herself that this is only one event, not a
major crisis. She needn't make it something bigger than it is.
She takes a slow, deep breath and greets Mrs. Jones with a
relaxed and positive attitude, ready for constructive problem
solving.

Controlling Emotions

Some school leaders stifle their emotions. They analyze problems objectively and respond without allowing their emotions to govern them. They appear to be model professionals. However, stifled frustrations mount throughout the day, simmering beneath their smiles. Finally, the emotions erupt, landing on any person unlucky enough to be present.

Gene is cool, calm, collected, and charming at school. When he reaches home, however, he unleashes the frustrations of the day. His bewildered family bears the brunt of his explosive tirades. Marsha is reserved and pleasant most of the time. Every now and then, however, she alarms the staff by exploding into anger over something that appears relatively trivial. Both she and Gene could spare other people needless misery by releasing their emotions in an acceptable form when they occur. Stockpiling feelings and acting them out in the wrong settings damage relationships and careers.

Keeping Focused

Administrators are easily distracted by interruptions, ideas, and emotions interjected by others. Young (1998) referred to this as an interaction-based response. Consider Tom's situation:

Despite his innovative ideas, Tom's meetings are seldom productive. His staff complains about rambling and unfocused discussions. He is often sidetracked and digresses into a discussion unrelated to the meeting's agenda. Distracted by visitors and phone calls, tasks lie unfinished on his desk; he loses things in the mounting stacks of papers.

To avoid being unfocused, keep a daily list of prioritized goals on your desk. When you're interrupted, tell people what you are doing and how much time you have to spare. During meetings, keep a written goal in view to keep you on your task.

One high school principal explained how he handled interrupted paperwork:

I can be easily distracted. I can get my desk into a total mess. Every so often, I have a new resolution that I'm not going to let that happen. It works for a while, but it's pretty hard in this job not to have things pile up. To take one thing and deal with it, put it to the side, and deal with the next isn't realistic in this job. But eventually, I go back and work it through. When I clear off my desk at the end of the day, everything I think was a priority for the day has been done.

FOCUSING ON SUCCESS

Success builds confidence while dwelling on failure erodes it.

—Denis Waitley

Pessimists are their own worst enemy. They dwell on every mistake instead of learning from them and moving forward. Everyone experiences days when nothing goes right and despair gains momentum. However, we can prevent a downward slide by thinking of past successes.

As an antidote for down days, some school leaders keep a folder of their accomplishments. Taking stock of what you have accomplished reinforces self-confidence.

The array of contents might include

- A curriculum vitae listing accomplishments
- Thank-you notes from parents and teachers
- Letters and pictures from students
- Certificates and awards
- Newspaper clippings
- Photographs
- Articles you have written
- Conference presentations you have made

When you need an attitude adjustment, take out the folder and enjoy reliving your successes. They will reenergize you and boost your self-confidence.

One elementary principal said,

I keep a folder in my desk drawer containing thank-you notes from parents, students, teachers, and colleagues. Whenever I'm discouraged, especially after someone complains or criticizes me, I open the folder. It reminds me of the good that I have accomplished and the appreciation of others; it encourages me to keep going.

Other school leaders keep a journal of their experiences. Recording feelings and events provides stress relief and also a record of past successes. Often problems become clarified and solutions more evident once they are written. One high school principal explained,

When problems occur, I tend to forget how much I've accomplished. Instead, the enormity of the problem at hand seems overwhelming. When I look back through my journal, I'm reminded of the relatively minor nature of this problem compared to the many successes that I've had. Also, by writing down the problem, it helps me clarify the core issues and sort out possible solutions.

Visualizing Success

Star athletes often say that they practice as much in their imagination as they do on the field. They have harnessed the tools of visualization and affirmation and rehearse a behavior until it seems automatic.

The power of visualization and affirmation are also used by successful school leaders. Janet, an elementary principal, described how she prepared for meetings with dissatisfied parents:

The night before the meeting, I find a quiet place and rehearse the meeting. I decide what I will say and imagine how the parents will respond. Then I practice the meeting in my mind until I feel comfortable and confident. I visualize myself calm and smiling. Just before the meeting the next day, I recapture the scene in my mind and tell myself that this will be a good meeting.

A high school principal reported that he regularly "talked to himself," reminding himself of traits that he wants to display such as "I am open to listening to parent concerns" before a difficult encounter.

Other leaders post messages to themselves as reminders. One elementary principal, who knew she needed to relax more, posted a message at home that said, "Time spent with cats is never wasted."

SUMMARY

Stress may originate from attitudes, perspectives, and ill-suited career or life choices. Rather than seeking external changes, it is more productive to alter personal attitudes, perspectives, and behaviors.

Develop a personal goal statement that reflects your personal vision and values. Translate your goals into specific plans of action.

Learn to do one thing at a time and enjoy the pleasure of each moment. Taking life at a slower pace requires practice, but the rewards include greater enjoyment and better health. The next chapter focuses on how you can alter your personal behavior to reduce stress.

CHAPTER FOUR

Housebreaking the Dragon:

Altering Personal Behaviors

I'm like a duck, swimming calmly on the surface, but paddling like hell under the water.

—A high school principal

Stress is seldom attributed to a simple cause, but rather to an accumulation of issues occurring at the intersection of our private and work lives. Stress attributed to work may stem primarily from home and be only secondarily related to work. Therefore, identifying and altering personal stress-producing behaviors is a necessary step in stress reduction.

Envision yourself walking a tightrope while carrying a tray of rubber balls that represent your health, spirituality, family, friends, and work. Keeping yourself and the tray balanced and upright are essential to a well-ordered life. The slightest imbalance could spill the tray's contents. While some contents are resilient enough to bounce back, others would be difficult to retrieve, and a few could be lost. A fall from the tightrope would be calamitous.

41

TAKING CARE OF YOURSELF: HEALTH AND SPIRITUALITY

The order of the tray's contents is by deliberate design. The stability of each relies on the stability of its predecessor. Health and spirituality are first, because they are essential to well-being. We must take care of ourselves first before attempting to take care of another. As we are reminded on airline flights, "First secure your own oxygen mask before assisting your child or someone else." One elementary principal explained, "I love my family, but I need to take care of myself. I'm number one."

Good health is critical. Health can be permanently damaged. Stress and physical deterioration combine to form a vicious cycle. While deterioration and illness increase susceptibility to stress, stress contributes to continuing deterioration and illness. Preventative measures must be taken to avoid the creation of a whirlpool effect (Willings, 1992).

Diet

Good nutrition is fundamental to good health and stress tolerance. A healthy diet is essential to maintaining the body's optimum functioning. When the body is deprived of basic nutrients, it is incapable of sustaining major stress and is susceptible to health breakdowns. The saying "We are what we eat" is true. Poor nutrition remains a problem in modern society despite the legions of books on nutrition that line bookstore shelves. We are a society that reads about nutrition while munching on snack foods. A typical comment from a principal was "I need to watch my diet carefully, as I tend to eat more when I feel stressed."

Proper nutrition and weight management are essentials. A simple formula, suggested by Creagen (1999), could be used to determine your adequate daily calorie count. Multiply your weight in pounds by 10. For instance, an adequate diet for someone weighing 150 pounds is 1,500 calories. Decreasing or increasing calories causes a loss or gain in weight. Creagen also recommended that a maximum of one third of the calories should be derived from fat.

Keep a food and beverage diary for a week. Record everything you consume throughout each day. Then analyze the pattern of your consumption and nutrition.

Exercise

Most people in the United States avoid exercise. We read books on exercise and join expensive health clubs, yet seldom walk anywhere. The drive-up conveniences of banks, pharmacies, car washes, and fast-food establishments are a testimony to U.S. lifestyles. The parking space closest to the door is prized. An out-of-service elevator is a crisis. A lost television remote control has the power to paralyze families. Rakes have been replaced with leaf blowers.

A frequent excuse for lack of exercise is lack of time. Women additionally complain that hair and makeup issues make it difficult for them to exercise. One female administrator explained,

I would love to be able to work out at noon like the guys. However, redoing my hair and makeup after exercising takes too long, . . . creates too many hassles. The same thing happens in the morning. If I exercise for an hour, then shower, dress, and do makeup and hair, have breakfast, and drive a half hour to work, I would need to get up at 4:30 a.m. That isn't realistic.

Yet, time spent on exercise actually reduces stress and contributes to higher productivity. School leaders who value the benefits of exercise find time to accommodate some form of exercise. One female administrator reported, "I do 80 sit-ups every morning." Another reported, "I work out in an exercise class three times a week. It's my salvation. I can tell the difference if I miss one. Regular exercise is very important to how I feel." Another reported, "I exercised more in the earlier years—out of vanity. I wanted to look good, so I watched what I ate and went to a health club. I haven't done as well lately, but I still walk a half hour every day." One male administrator reported, "I run four or five times a week and enjoy participating in triathlons. If I didn't engage in physical exercise, I know I would have suffered more effects from stress."

Exercise is one of the best stress-reduction techniques available. Exercise improves health, relaxes tense muscles, and promotes restful sleep.

One way to offset the inactivity of modern life is by incorporating walking into daily activities. For instance, get out of the car and walk to a destination. Park at the edge of the parking lot. Climb the stairs. Walk to the TV and turn it off. Fill TV time with activity rather than inactivity.

Walking for a designated period each day provides a simple and inexpensive exercise. Two hundred minutes of regular exercise per week is recommended. Walking for 20 to 30 minutes each day would achieve that goal (Creagen, 1999). Aerobics classes, running, and swimming can provide similar benefits.

An added benefit is derived from weight lifting for men and women. Lifting weights on alternate days strengthens muscles and helps prevent osteoporosis. It must be stressed, however, that the amount of weight and the kind of lifting should be appropriate for the individual (Creagen, 1999). Guidance from your physician and an exercise professional is recommended prior to beginning a weight-lifting program.

Before undertaking significant changes in diet and exercise, you should consult a physician. Equally essential prior to launching a program is having accurate and timely information on proper nutrition and exercise. Check with your physician, find a reputable and current source for advice, and have a customized exercise plan developed. Be sure that you select an exercise that you enjoy, so that you stick with it. Begin slowly, increase gradually, and be patient. Steps in developing an exercise regime include

- Checking with your physician
- Consulting reputable exercise professionals
- Developing an enjoyable and manageable program
- Beginning slowly
- Not expecting immediate transformation
- Sticking with it

Your health is your responsibility. No one else knows exactly how you feel or has the same level of concern. Working despite illness may be viewed favorably by your superiors, but they will not suffer the consequences of your poor health. You will. One elementary principal learned this lesson the hard way:

> I didn't miss a day despite being ill for most of the school year. I felt terrible, but continued to work, even weekends, to help with a special project. It was expected. . . . Nobody seemed to care that I should have been home in bed. When I left the school, I realized that I had been used. The project had been completed at the expense of my health.

Take proactive, preventative steps in safeguarding your health:

- Have regular physicals
- Become informed and proactive about your health care
- Make conscious and informed choices about what you consume
- Limit alcohol consumption
- Drink lots of water
- Exercise regularly
- Get enough sleep
- Take time off from work when you're ill

A combination of adequate rest, proper nutrition, regular exercise, and appropriate medical care can result in a healthier lifestyle.

FEEDING THE SPIRIT

What a commentary on our civilization when being alone is considered suspect; when one has to apologize for it, make excuses, hide the fact that one practices it—like a secret vice.

—Anne Morrow Lindberg (1983, p. 50)

Spiritual endurance comes from having a sense of purpose in life, being engaged in a cause beyond ourselves. A sense of inner calm and peace prevails.

People who give of themselves without replenishing sooner or later have little left to give. They experience spiritual poverty (Barrentine, 1993). The effects of spiritual poverty are subtle but are as debilitating and destructive as the physical wasting away of the body.

Despite this, some administrators have difficulty justifying a gift of time for themselves. "Too much to do and no time," they say. Yet, if they truly believed in its value, they would find a way to work time for themselves into their schedules.

Solitude rests the spirit, refreshes the soul, and reenergizes creativity. It is as important to mental health as diet and exercise are to physical well-being. Inner harmony radiates outward.

Enjoying solitude is a skill that must be relearned and practiced. After living with incessant noise, some individuals are no longer comfortable with solitude. Their need for noise is so ingrained that the absence of noise is distressing. They fill the quiet with music and television as background noise.

With practice, quiet solitude becomes a valued part of the day. A sense of serenity is achieved, one that remains a faithful companion upon reentry into the mayhem of life.

As one elementary principal said,

> I had to have a quiet time for myself. However, with a family, I couldn't do that until they were all asleep. Luckily, I'm a night person, so I got in the habit of going to bed at 2 a.m. Between the time my family went to bed and 2 a.m. became my quiet time. If I wasn't working on school-related things (sometimes I saved things that needed concentration to do until then), I'd read for enjoyment, do something I felt was relaxing. Believe it or not, some of the school-related things I was doing were relaxing because I had no interruptions, . . . for instance, budgets and paperwork that I couldn't get done at school.

One high school principal used evening quiet time to prepare for the next day. "I spend quiet time in the evening reflecting on how I'll respond to an impending situation so I can appear calm and collected the next day." An elementary principal found solace in prayer: "I have a book of meditations that I read from each day."

A strong spiritual life serves as an antidote to stress. While strategies such as prayer, meditation, reading, creating, or listening to music are commonly used, no one source of spiritual renewal is right for everyone. The answer lies in discovering a personal solution and making it part of a regular routine. One principal's solution: "I love to bake. So I bake things. . . . The faculty are the recipients. Sometimes I just hang out, do nothing. . . . I enjoy being alone." A high school principal said, "I find satisfaction in going to the garage and changing the oil in all the cars. There's a sense of completing something. I also enjoy caring for my lawn—it's relaxing."

Relaxing activities vary for each individual. Typical activities include

- Reading
- Playing with a pet
- Running
- Biking
- Playing the piano
- Gardening
- Painting

- Cooking
- Building
- Collecting
- Riding a horse
- Hiking
- Gardening

Spiritual renewal requires changing from the inside out. Sometimes it means letting go of old ideas and replacing them with new ones. Consider the parable of the teacher whose student asked her to teach him more. The teacher told the student to add more tea to an already full teacup. Obviously, the tea ran over the edges of the cup, as it could contain no more (Barrentine, 1993). Although it's difficult to let go of past beliefs, sometimes this is necessary for renewal.

Simplifying Your Life

One such belief is the notion in the United States that *more is better*. We are obsessed with acquiring "stuff," equating material possessions with happiness. Who we are is defined by what we have.

Rather than being fulfilling, however, an accumulation of material objects can become overwhelming. The accumulated stuff, as comedian George Carlin dubbed it, must be fixed, replaced, stored, organized, cleaned, moved, and safeguarded.

Life is easier when we're not overwhelmed by a clutter of possessions. Simplifying life by eliminating possessions can contribute to a sense of control and serenity. Lindberg (1983) called it "the art of shedding" (p. 30) and suggested, "Ask how little, not how much, can I get along with. Say, Is it necessary? when I am tempted to add one more accumulation to my life, when I am pulled toward one more centrifugal activity" (p. 35). One solution is to get rid of things you no longer use or need and stop buying more. One female administrator suggested, "Whenever you purchase something, make it a rule to recycle or dispose of another." A simplified lifestyle is less time consuming, less distracting, and brings with it a sense of order and serenity.

A second myth is *living for the future.* Individuals endure today in preparation for some future event—a career step, salary advancement, degree, vacation, or retirement. Life is perceived as waiting to happen or is still in the planning stages. Like the harried White Rabbit in *Alice's Adventures in Wonderland,* they are in a perpetual race to meet a deadline. Meanwhile, the present is lost. Irreplaceable moments of life slip away, unappreciated.

Learning to Relax

Achieving a state of relaxation is not always easy. Despite a desire to relax, tense muscles do not always cooperate. Learning simple relaxation exercises can help. Books and tapes that teach relaxation techniques are available. In addition, classes in practices such as yoga and tai chi provide opportunities for individuals who seek more structured experiences.

Some principals set aside a few minutes each day to relax. They shut the door, turn off the light, lean back in their chair, and close their eyes. A few minutes of breathing deeply and relaxing the neck and shoulders and they are more energized to face the rest of the day. One high school principal said, "I take a mental break by thinking about an upcoming trip or anticipating a dinner with my spouse that evening."

Progressive muscle relaxation is a technique used to relax each muscle in the body. Each muscle group is tightened and relaxed in a head-to-toe sequence. Books and tapes are available for those interested in learning the process. Sessions using tape-recorded instructions are an especially effective procedure.

A quick and easy method to relax tense muscles during a workday is to periodically ask, "Where am I feeling tense?" Notice a wrinkled brow, clenched teeth, a rigid neck, and raised shoulder muscles. Unfurl the brow, unclench the teeth, drop the shoulders, and move your head gently from side to side, up and down. This simple process is a quick way to relax the upper body, often the first to tighten under pressure. One administrator reflected, "I don't think I allowed my shoulders to drop until spring."

Other individuals use visualization techniques. They picture themselves at a favorite place experiencing the sounds, smells, and sensations. For sleepless worriers, visualization provides a safe alternative to sleeping pills. One high school principal said, "When I can't sleep, I picture myself at my favorite ocean resort, walking along the beach, with gentle waves washing over my feet. I feel the refreshing coolness of the trade winds and the warm sand under my feet."

Balancing Life and Work

The opposite principles of yin and yang in Chinese cosmology serve to illustrate the importance of balance in personal and professional lives. However important your work is, it constitutes only one portion of your life. A full life requires work that is balanced with family, friends, and outside interests.

Individuals whose careers are synonymous with their identities suffer loss of self-esteem when they leave their jobs due to retirement or illness. Although a career span is ordinarily finite, leaving a few years for retirement, some individuals behave as though their careers will last forever. They fail to prepare for the possibility or eventuality that they will no longer run a school or school district. One high school principal explained, "I can't imagine not being a principal, not working. I like what I do and don't know if I can be happy if I retire. What will I do? My friends are all colleagues and my social life revolves around my work."

The world's greatest leaders understood the need to escape from the world to become refreshed and renewed. Engaging in satisfying leisure activities is an effective deterrent to burnout (Stanton-Rich & Iso-Aloha, 1998).

Balancing life with other interests not only embellishes the present but also is a wise preparation for retirement. Create a list of things you enjoy. Each week include some items from this list on your schedule.

Creating Priorities for a Private Life

For zealous school leaders, work encroaches on family life. School events and evening meetings leave little time for family. When they are home on rare evenings, phone calls and briefcases full of work take precedence over conversations with their partners and children. Work left behind or in an untouched briefcase preoccupies their thoughts and dominates family conversations. Guilt over unfinished tasks overshadows the pleasure of being home. In the worst scenario, work-related frustrations and anger are inflicted on family members.

Spouses are left alone to raise children with little support. Some spouses resent the loss or neglect of their career due to the necessity of filling in for their absent partner. Marital relationships are strained when a spouse feels less important than a job (Bruckner, 1998).

Hectic days and evening meetings leave administrators with little of themselves to give on reaching home. They feel out of control, powerless in the face of the endless demands of work and home.

Making changes to accommodate our home life can restore a sense of personal power and control (Brock & Grady, 2000; Maslach, 1982). If spending time with the family is important and personally satisfying, then you need to channel time into this pursuit. Establishing a balance between giving and getting, stress and calm, work and home can be achieved by saying no to things that get in the way of family goals (Maslach, 1982).

One high school principal spoke of regaining a home life:

My spouse and I are both educators, so we used to take our problems home. We hashed out everything that went wrong at work. But now we simply ask, "How was your day?" After a few comments, we move on to other things. While we may discuss larger issues related to the field, we do not discuss day-to-day problems that occurred at our work sites.

An elementary administrator said, "I leave school problems at school. My spouse, also a school administrator, and I believe it's important to leave work problems at work. Although sometimes it's a relief to go home and talk about it, it's not fair to kids and spouse to continually bring your school problems into their home."

A high school principal reported, "I never take schoolwork home. And when I get home, I don't discuss school problems. I don't want to have a discussion of unpleasant issues. I disliked the situation at the time it occurred, and I certainly don't want to rehash it at home."

Consider the following:

- Schedule time for your family on your calendar, just as you do for any important group that wants to meet with you. These are the people who will be with you long after this job and your career have ended. They deserve your time and attention more than anyone else.
- Create a period of transition time between work and home. This is the time when you wrap up the day and plan for tomorrow.
- Leave the briefcase at work.
- If you must talk about work with your family, keep it brief and to the point and move on to something else.
- Plan activities at home that provide relaxation and fun.
- Plan weekly private times and dates with your spouse.
- When you're home, be fully present. The most important people in your life deserve your very best.

Protect, nurture, and treasure your family relationships. These are the people who love you, with whom you can be yourself. They provide an identity that surpasses professional roles. One high school administrator said, "I enjoy e-mailing my brother and grown children. Like letters of yesterday, e-mail keeps us in touch." Strong family ties are an effective antidote to stress.

Changing Gender Roles

Women ... must be open to all points of the compass: husband, children, friend, home, community; stretched out, exposed, sensitive like a spider's web to each breeze that blows, to each call that comes.

—Anne Morrow Lindberg (1983, p. 45)

Norms and Role Conflict

Traditional normative expectations for gender roles assign women as primary caretakers of home and children. Although normative changes continue to occur, it commonly remains the standard for gender role assignments. Those who adopt new norms feel judged by traditional norms. Role conflict abounds (Gmelch & Torelli, 1994).

Women with administration careers require cooperation from husbands in sharing household and child-rearing duties. Women's careers need to be perceived as equally important to their spouses. Marital conflict arises when the husband is unwilling to share responsibilities or perceives his career as more important than his wife's.

A Partnership

In a marriage in which the husband perceives himself as an equal partner in family responsibilities, the woman experiences less stress. As one female administrator reported, "I have a wonderful supportive spouse. We share equally."

Another noted, "If someone was of the old school, expecting you to be there every night and have a nice dinner on the table, it would be a problem. . . . This job doesn't contribute to that."

Shooting Yourself in the Foot

Some women create their own role conflict. They profess one thing while believing another. They verbalize equal partnership with their spouse but continue to believe that they are primarily responsible for home and children. Consequently, they experience personal guilt and disapproval, whether real or imagined. As one principal pointed out, "No matter what you say, if the house is in disorder, it still reflects on the woman. When the kids are sick, the school calls me, not him. The mother is responsible."

Having It All

Choices regarding the timing of children and the assumption of a leadership position are important. Women who mix administrative careers, pregnancy, and childbirth bear a heavy load. However helpful, a supportive spouse cannot override the physical and emotional demands of pregnancy and childbirth mingled with those of administration. Timing is the key to having it all and doing it well (Gallagher, 2000).

One female administrator explained her choices:

When my children were young, I was administrator of an elementary school and I had summers off. I didn't take a position in a high school until my children were nearing high school graduation or already in college. Unless your children were at the same school where you worked, it would be extremely difficult. You really wouldn't be able to be the kind of parent most of us would expect to be.

Partnerships at Home

Women and men with careers and families must decide what is essential and discard the rest. While some parents fret about mixing dual careers and child raising, one high school principal observed, "Your children grow up accepting as normal whatever you do. If you eat out a lot, it's normal to them. If you don't, that's normal too. It's what you're raised with."

One principal relayed a creative solution for meals: "One of the best things I did was assign each of the kids a night to cook, once they were old enough. It didn't matter what they fixed—hot dogs or macaroni and cheese out of the box. They got to have what they wanted, and I had dinner cooked. Sometimes we just went out for dinner. That's how we survived."

Other suggestions offered by principals include

- Hiring responsible child care (you can't concentrate on work if you're worried about your children)
- Seeking assistance if you're caring for an elderly parent
- Hiring someone to handle major housework and yardwork
- Dividing the duties of child care equally; set a schedule so each partner knows who is in charge during a particular period
- Dividing household duties; set a schedule and post it
- Delegating some household duties to children
- Giving up on routine but noncritical household tasks
- Considering long-range career goals in light of your spouse's goals as well as family circumstances

- Limiting the hours you spend at work; set a time when you leave for the day
- Setting time aside for yourself every day
- Setting aside one evening each week for a quiet dinner and time alone with your spouse; don't allow anything, short of a family emergency, to interfere
- Reserving weekends for family
- Attending functions related to your spouse's job

Handling Serious Problems

Some family issues are serious enough to dramatically increase stress levels at home as well as at work. Personal or family illness, death of a loved one, relationship problems, chemical dependency, difficulties with children, and financial problems are examples. These issues should be recognized and addressed as serious, stress-producing occasions that require attention. As one principal noted,

> These jobs do not have room for personal problems or stress beyond school issues. To add a personal crisis into a 13-hour day already packed full of problems . . . talk about stress. That would do it.

One high school principal observed,

> My father was in the hospital for several months before he passed away. To go to that hospital every night and visit was tremendously, tremendously stressful. There isn't time in these jobs for that.

Another elementary administrator found support from people at work:

> When I first started this job, I experienced a series of tragedies, one after another. I felt like a black cloud was hovering over me. I couldn't put the sadness aside when I came to work. I'm not good at that. But sometimes you have to do what you have to. The people here at school helped me, while dealing with their own problems. The kids helped as well.

There's nothing like being around children. . . . When you've had a lot of sadness in a short time, you figure out what's important in life.

Occasionally, the stress of a private problem interferes with work and productivity. Continuing to work at a stressful job when you're personally ill or consumed with worry or grief is most difficult. In addition, the extreme stress of a leader is contagious, contributing to increased incidences of stress and burnout of staff (Brock & Grady, 2000).

Administrators do not like to publicly acknowledge weakness or admit needing help. "Any show of weakness is an invitation for detractors to attack our Achilles heel" (Domenech, 1996, p. 41). However, taking a leave of absence or obtaining professional assistance may be a necessity.

SHARING TIME WITH FRIENDS

Your time is precious. Spend it with people who matter to you. Consider which friendships and relationships are important to you. Focus on maintaining them. Share time with friends.

Attending social outings to network with colleagues is not the same as socializing for relaxation. Although networking with colleagues is important, this should not be the basis of a social life. Having friends apart from work provides opportunities to reframe our outlook and perspective, to gain new ideas and view our situation in another context, and to relax and have fun.

Friends are the people who value you, rather than your job or what you can do for them. These are the people who will remain with you long after a particular job has ended and your career is over. While long-term friendships are formed at work, some friendships are based purely on mutual job interests. Some friends from work will remain lifelong friends, others will not. An enduring friendship includes factors other than work.

Comments about friends and colleagues include the following:

I often meet with colleagues from work. We've laughed over the years and said, "When we don't have these jobs anymore, we're going to have to get some friends."

Friendships are important to me. I like one-on-one relationships more than being in huge groups. I like to take long weekends to visit friends.

My friends right now are the parents of students with whom I socialize after games. The people we go to the playhouse and on our trips with are colleagues and parents. It's an interesting combination of parents of students who happen to be colleagues. There's a definite connection between work and social life because you don't have that much opportunity to socialize.

I have a network of friends from college. We get together several times a year, and that's a strong association. And we socialize with a neighborhood group, but they're all on a regular sort of functional basis.

Enjoying Leisure Time

What do you do when you're not working? Some administrators can't answer that question because they don't have any leisure time. They work long days, go to bed, and repeat the same schedule day after day. Work consumes every waking moment. Private and professional lives blur. One high school administrator explained,

When I first took this job, I had two or three evening type of activities with couples, gold league, and bridge groups. I found that I just couldn't get to them. There were too many things going on at work. After a time, I became very resentful that I had to drop those activities. But after a while I found it was really fun to go out with parents after games. . . . I found that my real choice today is to do just that. I've made this my social life along with my professional life and I like it. That's one of the reasons it would be real hard to give up this job.

Obviously, for administrators, especially those with families, time is limited. However, everyone needs some time to relax and some pursuit that promotes relaxation. Guard your private time as precious and savor every moment.

Sharing Life With a Pet

At the mention of a pet, the principal beamed, visibly relaxing, "Yes," she replied, "a little dog named Sassy. She is *soooo* wonderful, always waiting to greet me, tail wagging, wiggling with delight. It's a highlight in my day. Granted, her care takes a bit of time, but it's worth it."

Never underestimate the power of a pet. They bring us back to reality and shower us with unconditional love. History and literature are replete with examples of the animal-human bond. Emily Dickinson found refuge from the world in her Newfoundland dog Carlo (Adams, 1999). Feline admirers find comfort and emotional support from their cats, forging a bond not easily replaced by humans (Stammbach & Turner, 1999).

Physiological benefits of having pets include stress reduction, lowered blood pressure, and feelings of comfort. A case in point is the number of fish aquariums in doctors' waiting rooms (Eckstein, 2000).

Pets, however, require care and attention, both of which compound a busy schedule. Pet lovers deem it time well spent. As one high school principal said, "My little dog adds a certain amount of stress in that I have to show up to let her out and feed her. So I grumble a bit . . . but she's really worth it." Another said, "I like having pets and miss taking my dog for walks. He died last year. I'm looking forward to summer when I can get another dog."

However, one person's delight is another person's demon. People group around two positions regarding pets—those who love having them and those who don't. As one administrator pointed out, "I don't like pets. I don't want one."

People who are not pet lovers experience stress from the care, maintenance, and inevitable misdeeds and mishaps that accompany pet companionship. Having a pet is like living with a perpetual two-year-old. They never grow up and they never leave home. But if you enjoy animals, share your life with a pet. Their unconditional love and companionship negates the burden of their care.

MAINTAINING GOOD HEALTH

Sleep, exercise, and nutrition are essential to both good health and good spirits. When you're worn down and feeling sick, both work and personal life suffer. Yet, personal health is something often taken for granted or neglected. Proper diet, adequate rest, and regular exercise are necessary to maintaining good health.

Equally essential is spiritual growth. We each possess a core set of values that guide our lives. Periodically, we need to reconnect with this spiritual dimension. However you choose to fulfill the need for spiritual growth, be sure to schedule time for it on a regular basis.

Establishing a balance between work and home is achieved by saying no to things that get in the way of family goals and yes where it matters. Administrators with families must determine what is essential and discard the rest. Spend time with friends.

SUMMARY

Identifying and altering personal stress-producing behaviors are necessary steps in stress reduction. Good health is critical. A healthy diet and regular exercise are essential to good health.

Solitude rests the spirit, refreshes the soul, and reenergizes creativity. Enjoying solitude is a skill that must be learned and practiced.

Balancing a work life and a private life is challenging. Making changes to accommodate a home life can restore a sense of personal power and control. Women and men with careers and families must decide what is essential and discard the rest. Capitalizing on work stress is the subject of the next chapter.

CHAPTER FIVE

Harnessing the Power:

Capitalizing on Work Stress

Experience is the best teacher. I learned not to worry, gave up perfectionism, and became more realistic in expectations for myself and others.

—An elementary school principal

RECOGNIZING EXCESS STRESS

Time spent at work occupies a major portion of administrators' waking hours. Few limit their workweek to 40 hours. The nature of this fast-paced, multifaceted job subjects administrators to prolonged periods of stressful activities. It is common for administrators to be unaware of the extent of their work-related stress, often ignoring physical manifestations and deteriorating relationships.

For some administrators, an addictive quality to the fast pace of administrative life is the adrenaline rush that comes with challenges, the satisfaction of success. They find the stress stimulating. As one high school principal explained, "I like the fast pace—probably because I've been in a fast pace for so long that I wouldn't know any better. It's the high-paced nature of the work, the adrenaline that keeps you going. I worry about how I'll adjust if one day I don't have this fast pace."

For these individuals, the fast pace is difficult to abandon, even for a vacation. One high school administrator recalled a family vacation: "It took me two of the three days to get to a point where I could stop scheduling everyone and everything. Finally, my children suggested that I stop planning things, go lie in the sun, and enjoy. That part of being used to working at a certain level—it takes a while to calm down."

Some administrators are working at their comfort level. They perceive their work as challenging. As one elementary principal observed, "I'm comfortable here. This school is easy for me to handle, yet presents enough challenges to keep me interested."

Some administrators feel overburdened with stress at work. They struggle to maintain high productivity despite the stress. Reluctant to ask for assistance and fearing being perceived as weak or lacking leadership ability, they silently endure the stress despite the erosion of their health and relationships. They refuse to acknowledge, perhaps even to themselves, the suffering they endure.

Individuals who care about their work and set high standards for themselves run the highest risk of stress and burnout. They are usually high achievers who demand great things of themselves, never feel satisfied that they are doing enough, and overwork until they are exhausted. Perfectionists are often found in this category.

Administrators need to examine the stress in their job as well as their responses to that stress. Consider your ideal level of stress. Plot your current stress level on a scale of 1 to 10, with 1 indicating no stress and 10 indicating burnout. To find out how others perceive you, ask someone close to you to identify your stress level. One high school principal who said she suffered little stress, probably a level 3, was shocked when her spouse reported her stress as high, between 5 and 8.

Identifying Causes

Administrators report that stress emanates primarily from day-to-day situations such as multiplicity of roles, time constraints, work overload, an unrelenting pace, fragmentation and brevity of work, continual shifting of gears, interpersonal conflicts, isolation, and organizational structures. In some cases, gender and race are additional factors (Pigford & Tonnsen, 1993).

As the array of people, events, and situations increases, so too does the potential for stress. Issues include pressures for accountability, mandates for higher standards, lack of recognition, changing social values, and the decline of the traditional family structure (Brock, Ponec, Hamman, Nelson, & Goff, 1996; Whitaker, 1996). One high school principal explained, "I feel the effects of larger issues, such as mandated testing, state finance issues, but not in the same sense of urgency as I do the day-to-day issues in the building."

Administrator stress is derived from the basic work components of role, task, organization, and human interaction. Common stressors include

- Time constraints
- Paperwork
- Variation of job responsibilities
- Telephone interruptions
- Visitor interruptions
- Parental complaints
- Parent groups
- Conflicts between parents and teachers
- Staff conflicts
- Student misbehavior
- Too many meetings
- Nighttime activities
- Making decisions that affect others
- Staff evaluations
- Unprofessional teachers
- Militant teachers
- Teacher apathy
- Negative staff members
- Inadequate performance of any employee
- Terminating teachers
- Writing critical evaluations
- Rumor control
- Assemblies
- Gaining community support
- Lack of support from superiors
- Unclear expectations
- Inadequate feedback
- Lack of parental support
- Poor facilities
- Lack of resources, supplies, funding
- Vandalism
- State and federal regulations
- Lack of social life
- Feelings of inadequacy
- Dissatisfaction with salary
- Lack of recognition
- Dissatisfaction with career advancement

Parochial Schools

Principals of parochial schools, funded by parish donations and tuition, report the following stressors:

- Financial difficulties, complicated by dependence on donations and tuition.
- Working for a superior (usually a priest) who has no expertise in administering schools. One principal said, "The person in control has no training, no background in education."
- The autonomous nature of parochial schools. One elementary principal explained, "I was the central office, writing all the curriculum and policies. I put the program together. There was no one to turn to for support."
- Lack of job security. Renewal of yearly contracts was determined by the parish priest and subject to pressure from parents and donors. One principal explained, "We're at the mercy of people who know nothing about what we do and who have complete control over whether or not we will have a job. . . . It's a popularity contest" (Brock & Fraser, 2001).

Principals who solved or circumvented these stressors reported long and fulfilling careers. Their suggestions include

- Ensuring compatibility with a pastor prior to accepting a position. Be certain the partnership will work before you take the job. People are usually on their best behavior during interviews and courtship. As in marriage, it is foolhardy to plan on a partnering improving after the contract is signed.
- When a change of pastor occurs, meet with the new pastor to discuss roles, responsibilities, and establish a structure for ongoing communication. The transition period is the optimal time to establish communication, clarify goals, and determine operating procedures (Brock & Fraser, 2001; Brock & Grady, 1995; Fraser, 1998). One principal's strategy is, "When new pastors arrive, I meet with them and tell them . . . since you inherited me, we need to get acquainted, discuss our respective roles, and decide how we want to make decisions. I let them know that I can't run the school without their cooperation."

- Obtain annual evaluations from the supervisor(s) or supervising body, as well as from the teachers. Respond to the recommendations.

Confronting Job Stress

To ameliorate stress, make changes in the situation. When stress is out of control, it may be difficult to decide what to change. A typical response is to blame someone or something else for the stress. An obvious example is beginning teachers who think their discipline problems will be solved by more rules, failing to see that their lack of classroom organization creates the problem. Instead, identify the nature of the problem, its level of importance, who owns it, and what changes or actions are necessary.

Some school stress may be idiosyncratic, but most situations have been encountered and solved by other administrators. Successful administrators report managing stress by

- Taking care of themselves (time alone, exercise, nutrition)
- Engaging in activities with family and friends
- Having and following an educational philosophy
- Having a clear understanding of their role
- Networking with colleagues
- Matching their leadership style to the needs of the school
- Learning not to wallow in worry
- Laughing and encouraging laughter at work
- Approaching conflicts as problems to be solved
- Focusing on issues they can control
- Knowing how to manage their time (prioritize, say no, and delegate)
- Having excellent interpersonal skills

Finding the Right Job Match

Role Conflict

Some administrators struggle to deal with differences between what they believe should be done and their employers' expectations. One high school principal said,

When I was hired, I was told to raise academic standards and improve the school's organization. Yet, teacher absenteeism is allowed and rampant (because of sick and personal days provided contractually), and too much class time is given up for nonacademic activities. Someone gave away the farm in this district and I don't have the authority to buy it back.

Administrators must be able to manage role conflict and ambiguity, or stress and emotional exhaustion will master them. One high school principal said, "This isn't a situation where I'm likely to stay a long time." Role conflict has a direct impact on job satisfaction, and unchecked, it is a potential cause of burnout.

Those considering a new administrative position should carefully examine the position in relation to their personal aspirations and philosophy. Gathering information about the philosophy and expectations of the school allows them to make an informed choice. If the job does not fit, or factions within the school disagree on goals, role conflict may create an untenable and career-damaging situation (Brock & Grady, 1995). A change of position may be the only alternative.

Clarify Your Role

Role Ambiguity. Administrators are expected simultaneously to be instructional leaders, change agents, and managers. Roles for school leaders are expanding. New societal issues have increased administrators' interactions with law enforcement, health, and social services agencies. Entering uncharted territory without previous training and experience contributes to role ambiguity. When roles are ambiguous, administrators may lack a sense of direction that results in stress and consequent feelings of depersonalization and a lack of personal accomplishment (Gmelch, 1994). As one administrator said, "I began to lose self-esteem and doubt the accuracy of my perceptions. I doubted my decisions because I couldn't please my superior to save my soul."

Support from one's supervisor reduces the feelings of stress caused by ambiguity and conflict (Gmelch, 1994). One administrator said, "I've been very blessed that the supervisors with whom I've worked have been very supportive. All 26 years of my career I was never asked to change a decision. I was backed 100 percent and never called on the carpet because of disenchantment with me or my decisions."

Leaders who struggle with role ambiguity frequently report receiving little or no feedback from supervisors. Remarks from administrators who struggled with role ambiguity include, "I've been here 10 years, and last year I had my first evaluation." "In 8 years, I never had an evaluation, not one. My supervisor was 99 percent absent from the environment, had no idea what the names of most of the staff were." Another reported, "My evaluations were sporadic; some years I received one and other years nothing."

To reduce role ambiguity, consider the following:

- Establish your own philosophy
- Identify your role
- Clarify priorities with your superior(s)
- Communicate regularly with your superiors
- Obtain periodic performance reviews

Separate Self From Work

School administrators identify closely with their work. Their behavior is determined by traits and attitudes necessary for job performance, and these traits are encouraged and reinforced. Those traits perceived as unnecessary are suppressed, and they gradually weaken. In a sense, individuality is stifled by the effort to mold the self to fit an administrative role in a particular organization (Carr, 1994).

Share Problems With Colleagues

The role of a school administrator is isolating. Without a point of reference, problems appear disproportionately unique, important, and unsolvable. The intensity of stress is usually matched by a tendency to withdraw from the people most equipped to provide assistance.

Having a network of people with whom to share problems, ideas, and successes is essential. Administrators need three kinds of support:

1. Trustworthy, confidential, and loyal people in the school with whom they can share and discuss (secretary, office

staff, key personnel). One elementary principal said, "I tell my troubles to my secretary. I don't want to let the teachers know when I'm concerned." A high school principal said, "Having a leadership team to discuss problems with is essential."

2. Colleagues in the field who share similar problems. One elementary principal said, "I have four close principal friends. We go out once a month and share problems and suggestions. We discuss personal and professional problems . . . and we know that none of what is said will be betrayed as a confidence. I've never felt that I had all the answers. . . . This really helps."

3. Social contacts, people who can provide support, comfort, advice, and laughter. One high school principal said, "Spending time with people outside the education world imparts a different perspective on your work. Problems seen in a wider context have a way of diminishing."

ADAPT TO THE SETTING

Toto, I've a feeling we're not in Kansas anymore.

—Dorothy *(The Wizard of Oz)*

Each work environment has a unique culture, community, and needs. Although it may be tempting to re-create the new workplace in the image of your previous one, it probably would not meet the needs of the community. In addition, an administrative style used effectively in one setting may be ineffective in another (Brock & Grady, 1995).

Principals described their adjustment issues:

When I first came to the new school, it wasn't unusual for a number of parents to let me know very strongly what their priorities and viewpoints were. So we had some getting used to. While I was impressed by the large number that attended the first PTA meeting that I attended, I later found out that they came to see the new principal. But now I have positive things to report about every parent—even those who were initially negative. We're found a way to work together.

When I first came here as a first-year principal, I had these idealistic ideas for creating a perfect school in a short period of time. Then reality tempered my thinking. I learned about this community, these people, and what they wanted and needed. I've made changes, but I've learned to bring the people with me—to work with them.

One elementary principal acknowledged, "In the least favorite of my three schools, I was in my first year of administration and only 26 years old. In retrospect, perhaps I could have learned to be a better match myself."

Stop Wallowing in Worry

Several principals reported that worry was a major source of stress in their early years of administration, but they learned to overcome it. One elementary principal commented,

I used to worry and fret about things that hadn't happened. But that was at a time when I thought I could control more than I can control. When you learn that you can't control everybody and everything around you, you just deal with it as it comes. I don't mean that I don't plan and do things proactively, but there are just some things, probably the biggest stressors, that you cannot deal with ahead of time. Part of it comes from the experience of worrying about things three weeks in advance and finding out that isn't what happened at all. Maybe it's just getting older and wiser, or having no time to worry. But it sure is a waste of time and energy. I sleep like a baby now.

Another high school principal observed, "Stress diminishes performance. I have seen it in leaders who just don't get things done. When you get right down to it, I think it's due to wallowing in worry, rather than taking the job, piece by piece, and getting it done."

I used to worry. But I gave it up when it didn't help. Now I do the best I can. The bottom line is what's best for the kids. If I do worry, it's about the students and some of their situations.

Focus on Issues You Can Change

Administrators feel frustrated when situations beyond their control affect their work. A principal in a large district explained, "Maintenance of this building is a source of stress for me. When something is dripping, needs to be fixed, and the person responsible has chosen other priorities, while people keep coming in to tell me it's still not fixed, . . . it causes stress."

If you can solve the situation, solve it. However, the only behavior you can change is your own. If you do not have the power to change a situation, such as an organizational structure, state mandates, or budget allotments, focus on what you can change. One public school administrator explained how she did that: "Lack of resources was a challenge. So we decided to write grants and fund-raise to obtain what we needed. It took a lot of hours but, nevertheless, the reward was when our teamwork paid off."

Rules and constraints are boundaries. You may not be able to change the boundaries, but you can find ways to work within them. In the words of poet Rick Masten,

> *a case of burnout demands a second opinion*
> *and this is mine*
> *find an outlet*
> *and if the cord doesn't reach*
> *move the set.*

Plan for Crisis

A school crisis is undoubtedly a source of stress. Recent school tragedies provide reasons for concern. In response, school administrators are implementing measures to ensure safety of students and staff. Peace of mind is predicated on preventative measures. Several researchers (Brock, Nelson, Grady, & Losh, 1998; Grady, 1995a, 1995b, 1996; Grady, Bendezú, & Brock, 1996; Grady,

Haar, & Losh, 2001; Grady, Krumm, & Losh, 1997; Losh, Krumm, Grady, & Brock, 1996) suggest that these measures include

- Providing a safe school environment
- Having a written crisis plan
- Assembling a crisis leadership team
- Periodically reviewing safety and crisis plans and responses with all staff—a plan is worthless unless the people who work in the building know and use it

However, crises are not always preventable. They can and do occur despite the best plans and preventative measures. As one high school principal said, "When you work with a large number of people every day, the possibility of crisis will always be there." This threat is an underlying and ever-present source of stress.

An administrator shared her coping and response strategies:

For sure, crises raise the adrenaline, but you deal with it. . . . At first, I used to think that when something occurred, it was my fault for not seeing it coming. Shouldn't I have been able to proactively do something about it? But when you deal with this many people, you come to understand, no, most things of a crisis level you probably couldn't have done anything about. You just need to handle them when they occur.

The first thing I do is call my leadership team together. Share the burden, the responsibility, and the ideas of what should be done. Every crisis is different. You can have all the plans in your crisis book, but in the end, you're going to deal, on that day, with this situation in a way that's reasonable, no matter what's written down. Having a leadership team is key. We do the best we can at that time and then go home and get a good night's sleep, exhausted.

Practice Androgyny

Develop a leadership style that uses the full repertoire of human behaviors. Individuals whose leadership style combines male and female behaviors, rather than gender stereotypical behaviors, experience less stress (Gmelch & Chan, 1997).

Overcome Discrimination

People of color, especially black women, often experience subtle and not so subtle forms of discriminatory behaviors. A multitude of issues may surface. You may be resented because you were selected for the job. Remind yourself that you were selected because you are more capable (Pigford & Tonnsen, 1993). Do not dwell on the resentments of others, because you cannot change how they feel or behave. Over time, your actions may change their perceptions.

If you are one of a handful of minorities in the district, you may be invited to be on more committees than you can handle. Be certain that your ideas, rather than your mere presence, are valued. Be selective in where you serve (Pigford & Tonnsen, 1993).

Regard the scrutiny of colleagues and parents as a rite of passage. Most new administrators are scrutinized. If you are of a different ethnic origin than the majority of parents in the school, the situation will likely intensify. One principal recalled, "There was standing room only at the first PTA meeting. I was on center stage. They all came to look me over."

Give people time to know you. Responding angrily or defensively will not help, and will likely make the situation worse. One principal shared her experiences:

Some parents let me know that black principals belonged in predominately black schools and white principals in white schools. When I was the principal of a primarily "white" school, a group of parents felt they didn't have to respect my authority. In their opinion, I was African American and didn't understand conditions or problems that affected Caucasian families.

Escape On and Off the Job

Finding solitude in a school, even for a few minutes, can be difficult. One elementary principal recalled a day of desperate measures: "I had a stream of visitors, each of whom had a crisis to impart. When I left to use the restroom, one mother trailed me into the ladies room and talked to me through the door of the stall."

Strive to escape from the people and demands for a few minutes. Schedule a quiet time each day when the door is closed, there are no calls or visitors, when you can lean back and relax. Some administrators do light exercises to reenergize. One principal did sit-ups in his office. Whatever your choice of activities, a daily time-out is a deterrent to burnout (Stanton-Rich & Iso-Aloha, 1998).

The business world rewards management with perks such as trips and retreats to exotic places, which does not usually happen in education. Some administrators' solution is to create their own perks. They reward themselves by planning minivacations. One high school principal explained, "My spouse and I plan dinner out twice a week. I look forward to that, knowing that I'll go out to dinner, have a glass of wine, and relax. Even if I have work to do later that evening, the break is helpful."

Another said, "We have two couple friends, both in this business, and we plan spring breaks together—a year in advance. Opportunities like that to totally get away, lie on a beach, do nothing, . . . just looking forward to that, having that thought in your mind is a break—a mental vacation."

One need not leave town to get away. Another administrator spends several weekends a year at a local hotel with her spouse. When you cannot get away for a weekend, try a minivacation or an afternoon alone doing something you enjoy. If you are married, pick a day when your spouse is working and the children are at school or day care. Turn off your cell phone and computer.

The measures need not be elaborate, but they need to be deliberate. Plan time away from the burdens of work. Anticipation of the event can be almost as relaxing and important as the event itself.

LAUGH AND ENCOURAGE LAUGHTER

He who laughs, lasts.

—Norwegian proverb

When all else fails, laugh. Humor, although often taken for granted, is an essential part of life. A phenomenon as old as humanity, the Bible mentions humor 29 times. As noted in Ecclesiastes 8:15, "Then I commended mirth because a man hath no better thing under the sun than to eat, and to drink, and to be merry" (Cornett, 1986).

A good laugh does make you feel better. It increases oxygen in the blood, exercises the lungs, diaphragm, and face muscles, causes the pulse to drop, and increases the production of endorphins. Tensions subside and remain lower after laughing (Cornett, 1986).

The sound of laugher resonated through the office walls. The high school principal commented,

> You'll hear a lot of laughter around here. The staff banter all day long. It's important, . . . a great stress reliever, as they are all facing time constraints and crunches, things they need to do for me and other people. At the end of the day, when you go through here, you would think that you've arrived at something less than a professional office because they're laughing so hard at something someone has said or they're giving someone a hard time.

The contraction of 15 facial muscles and assorted noises seems to serve no utilitarian purpose other than to make us feel relaxed and momentarily forget our problems (Cornett, 1986). That alone is of great value. Laughter can ease difficult, tense moments.

Humor can decrease tension and improve interpersonal relationships and the atmosphere of the workplace. People prefer being around people who smile and appear relaxed. One principal spoke of the effects of a smile: "I was leaving a business lunch with colleagues when our waiter surprised me by saying, 'Thank you for your smile. You made my day much brighter. Nobody else has smiled at me all day.'"

Lighten up. Assign less power to events. Learn to laugh at yourself and your situation. Humor provides comic relief and helps distance you from problems. Following are ways school leaders incorporate humor into their lives:

- Read cartoons and post your favorites in the office
- Include jokes and cartoons in employee newsletters

- Watch funny TV shows
- Go to humorous movies and plays
- Spend time with people who like to laugh
- Look for the funny side of annoying situations
- Draw cartoons of funny events
- Laugh with others, but never at them
- Include 5 full minutes of hearty laughter in every day

Administrators suggest the following:

- Don't take things so seriously. One principal joked, "I acquired a Ph.D. so I could open milk cartons in the cafeteria, distribute birthday treats, check for head lice, and dispense Band-Aids."
- Laugh at yourself. "When you get locked in the restroom and miss the end-of-the-year faculty luncheon, what else can you do . . . laugh."
- Encourage your staff to laugh. Joke with them.
- Share your sense of humor. Include jokes in the faculty bulletins.

One high school principal said, "At my previous job, I enjoyed the monthly principal get-togethers. We shared stories, common experiences that nobody else would understand, and laughed about things until tears rolled down our faces. Being with those who share identical experiences and being able to talk about them, . . . that was good medicine."

In the words of an anonymous author, "Humor is the hole that lets a little sawdust out of a stuffed shirt."

SUMMARY

Confronting job stress may require you to make changes at work. Managing stress is possible. Reducing role conflict and role ambiguity is essential. Develop a network of colleagues to reduce professional isolation. Laugh and encourage laughter, because humor can decrease tension and improve interpersonal relations and the atmosphere of the workplace. In the next chapter, we discuss effective time use.

CHAPTER SIX

Shrinking the Dragon

Using Time Effectively

We have only so many ergs of energy in the morning, and if we do not choose how to use them, they will evaporate like the morning dew.

—E. Creagan (1999, p. 49)

THE TIME CRUNCH

Time is a major issue for administrators. The pressure of time and the intensity with which administrators operate make them vulnerable to emotional exhaustion, the culprit most responsible for administrator burnout (Gmelch & Chan, 1994). According to administrators, "There's too much to get done and not enough time to do. . . . I'm always hurrying to get things done because there isn't any more time and the next thing is waiting . . . and the next thing is waiting."

Trying to get everything done, meeting everyone's needs, problems, paperwork, last-minute requests. . . . When you line up all the things to be done and look at an eight-hour day, it's really a joke. By the time you've ploughed through the day's problems and everyone clears out, people are arriving for evening events. If I don't have a Saturday to catch up, I find myself two weeks behind. I work Saturday, sometimes part of Sunday, usually six days a week, 13 hours a day. It's stressful. . . . I don't have enough personal time.

Few would dispute the staggering workload of school administrators. Given the number of hours in a day and the doubtful decrease in administrator demands, the only solution is to learn new ways of operating. To do so requires getting rid of old habits.

WORK OVERLOAD

I may look like I don't have a thing to do, but things are churning inside.

—A high school principal

Work overload refers to an excessive amount of work that an administrator is expected to accomplish in a given time. Each day consists of 1,440 minutes. If you have too many tasks and responsibilities, then something must be eliminated. Reshuffling the schedule is not the answer. Find things to remove and make changes in how you operate.

Factors that contribute to work overload include

- Revolving office door
- Poorly designed work space
- Lack of organization
- Cluttered office
- Lack of clear priorities
- Inefficient use of time
- Poorly trained office staff
- Uncooperative personnel
- Refusal to delegate
- Perfectionism
- Reluctance to share leadership
- Too many meetings
- Inability to say no
- Ineffective people skills

Consider reducing the quantity of work while retaining the quality. Often it is not the actual administrative tasks that are the problem, but rather allowing your time to be wasted.

Control Your Environment

Some time wasters are environmental stressors, most of which are under the control of the administrator. Environmental stressors decrease efficiency, creating a sense of frustration and work overload.

Environmental stressors in schools include poorly designed furniture, noise, dim lighting, crowded conditions, and for some administrators, the practice of leaving the office door open. People wander in, creating endless interruptions.

Stop interruptions by closing the door and scheduling time when you accept phone calls. Equip the office with comfortable furniture, suitable storage, appropriate technology, and adequate lighting. Arrange your furniture so you have privacy when you need it.

Organizing the Lair

Some administrators compound their stress by trying to work in rubble. Office organization and functionality either help or hinder work completion. Working in a well-organized office diminishes stress: hunting for things in a messy office generates frustration and compounds stress.

Organize paperwork so there is a place for everything. Some principals are notorious for losing things on their desks. Others live with mounds of papers stacked on the floor, insisting that they know right where everything is. A filing system is a better alternative.

Keep your desktop clean, occupied by only the items you are currently using. You will feel more in control if you are not visually reminded of multiple, pending demands. Some administrators use a colored folder system, such as red for priority items that require completion today, green for items due within the week, and blue for longer-term items.

The practice of handling a paper only once works. One high school administrator said, "When something hits my desk, I read it and handle it accordingly. I don't want things piling up. By the end of today, that stack of papers on my desk will be gone."

At the end of each day, clear the desktop except for your calendar and a list of priorities for the next day. Place unfinished work or long-term projects in a desk drawer, out of sight and out of mind until the next day.

Create an office environment that is functional, professional, attractive, and comfortable. You will feel more relaxed and in control. In addition, a tidy office projects a sense of professionalism that builds trust and tells visitors and personnel that you are in charge. This visual message influences impressions and future interactions.

Office desks and workspaces should provide privacy. However, many administrators like their offices situated so they can see who is entering the school and office. One elementary principal noted,

> I can never sit with my back to the door. I want to see who's coming in the office and, if possible, see who's entering the building. If the media, for example, are coming up the walk, I can duck out and give myself prep time while they go through the protocol of checking into the office. This is where it's important to have a good secretary. Secretaries can stall and buy you preparation time.

TRAIN OFFICE STAFF

If you want to survive, make sure you get along with your secretary and custodian.

—An elementary principal

A well-trained office staff can decrease an administrator's workload. As one elementary administrator pointed out, "My secretary is my most valuable ally." A well-trained school secretary can deflect nuisance calls and interruptions, subdue minor crises and distraught parents, and handle filing and correspondence, all the while providing comfort to sick students, upset parents, and disgruntled staff.

Administrators fortunate to have a full complement of office staff can reduce their workload immensely by assigning appropriate duties, followed by proper training and regular performance evaluations. Be clear about expectations and quick to recognize good performance.

Allow your office staff to run the office. One secretary lamented, "I could save him hours and hours of work if the administrator would only let me do my job."

Secure Cooperation of Maintenance Personnel

"What is my most frustrating problem?" echoed the principal. "Getting the janitor to clean the school!" When maintenance personnel are ineffective, an administrator's workload expands to solve the problem. Proper personnel selection, training, and performance reviews are the first step. In addition, letting personnel know the importance of their role in achieving school goals and including them in appropriate school discussions, decisions, and celebrations is vital. People who feel integral to the organization work harder.

DO IMPORTANT THINGS FIRST

The trick is not to work harder, but better.

—A high school principal

Some administrators are busy all day doing things that have little to do with school goals. Easily distracted, they use a firefighting approach, reacting to issues as they occur. At the end of the day, they feel frustrated, having accomplished little more than putting out fires.

Manage your time in relation to the importance of the tasks. Make a list of what you want to accomplish during the day. Make sure the tasks are important to the accomplishment of school goals. Keep the list short—three to five items—and allow for the inevitable emergency. Assume each item will take at least two or three times longer than you anticipate. After each interruption, return to your task list. Check off each completed task and move to the next item.

Determining priorities and working toward accomplishing those priorities provide a sense of accomplishment. When fires interrupt, they must be doused. Once the fire is extinguished, we must return to the priority task. One high school administrator pointed to a stack of papers on her desk. "My appointments and those folders contain today's priorities. Before I leave tonight, I will have handled today's essential tasks. Items that can wait will be carried over for tomorrow."

Stop Procrastinating

Do the toughest things first. If you put something off until the last minute, you deprive yourself of the time to do your best and to make improvements if needed. Procrastination not only increases your stress but also the stress of those who work with you.

Use But Don't Be Used by Technology

E-mail, faxes, and voice mail are efficient tools for communication. Used appropriately, they can speed administrators' work. Used indiscriminately, they can consume vast amounts of time.

How to control electronic communications:

- Consider limiting the distribution of your e-mail address
- Keep professional and personal e-mail on separate accounts
- Limit e-mail to school-related business, not jokes or cute stories
- Establish a time to respond to e-mail and voice mail, not several times a day and not from home
- Remember that whatever you say in an e-mail can be forwarded to hundreds of people with a single command

Establish a Schedule

Some tasks occur daily, for instance, greeting students and staff in the morning, reading and responding to mail, handling e-mail, monitoring hallways and the cafeteria, observing classrooms, returning phone calls, and dismissal procedures. Repetitious activities and their format vary according to school population and size, as well as the administrator's style and priorities. Regardless of the list, however, having a schedule for important but repetitious activities provides a structure around which to plan the day, week, and month.

Plan activities that involve people during times when people are present and paperwork when you are alone. If your main task is supervising instruction in the school, activities related to that function should be the focus of your time when students and staff are present.

Paperwork and report writing are best accomplished when the least number of people are in the building. One elementary principal observed, "I used to be annoyed when people interrupted my paperwork. I always stopped working and listened politely, but inside I was annoyed. Then one day I realized, 'This is what I'm supposed to be doing—helping and working with people. Paperwork can wait. People come first.'"

Minimize Socializing

Most people do not recognize the amount of time they spend socializing. Although it is important to spend time conversing with school personnel, students, and visitors, socializing can become a seductive time waster. Consider shortening the length of your hallway and phone conversations.

Schedule Appointments

Setting appointments for individual conferences enables you to control your time and schedule. In addition, the advanced warning gives you time to gather information. Allowing people to wander in and chat gives away your time and leaves you vulnerable to confrontations without preparation.

Let the visitor know the time frame of the meeting when the appointment is made. For instance, you can say, "I have an hour available Thursday afternoon. I can meet with you between 1:00 and 2:00 p.m." Keep the conversation focused on the topic. To signal the end of a meeting, summarize the discussion, organize your papers, and stand up. If issues remain, schedule another meeting. You could say, "I have another appointment now, but if you'd like, we can schedule another meeting."

Eliminate the Nonessential

Some repetitive tasks are done out of habit rather than because of their importance. Doing nonessential tasks can easily become a habit that consumes valuable time. Consider the repetitive tasks you perform on a daily, weekly, and monthly basis. Which ones do not contribute to goal accomplishment? If they are not linked to goal outcomes, they are not necessary. Eliminate nonessentials; save your time for important tasks. As one high school principal observed, "I discovered the need to prioritize. Some things just aren't that important. Some don't need to be done."

Sometimes a task is necessary, but given too much time. One elementary principal said, "I used to overprepare, I spent needless time on things that didn't deserve that much time. Now I've learned to do what needs to be done, but in moderation. The trick is not to work longer but to work better."

Eliminate Extraneous Meetings

Does this sound familiar: "I used to belong to an organization that held a meeting to plan the agenda and another meeting to plan for the meeting. The organization had assumed a life and importance of its own that superseded its original function—one that nobody remembered after a while."

Administrators frequently find themselves sitting through meaningless meetings. Even worse, sometimes they are guilty of scheduling unnecessary meetings.

Simplify your professional life. Eliminate unnecessary meetings, stop attending unnecessary functions, and resign from extraneous committees.

Meetings Versus Memos

The purpose of a meeting is to provide an opportunity for two-way communication. If your intention is to impart information without inviting input or questions from the participants, send a memo instead. Suggestions for a productive meeting include

- Distributing an agenda before the meeting
- Establishing a meeting length that is reasonable for the time of day and topic
- Notifying participants who will be asked to contribute information

- Adhering to the designated starting time
- Adhering to the agenda
- Inviting discussion within time limits
- Adhering to the designated ending time

Learn to Say No

If you say "yes" to everything, you are in effect saying "yes" to nothing.

—E. Creagan (1999, p. 49)

Successful people work hard doing the right things. When asked or invited to do something, consider your priorities and the school's goals. If the activity does not fit the goals, say no. Learn to say no to the wrong things; save your time for the right things. Be gracious, but firm "No, but thank you for the offer. I'm overcommitted at this time."

Learn to say no to other people's problems. Just because they dump problems on your desk does not mean that you must accept them. Acknowledge their problems and hand them back. Ask, "How do you think you can handle this?" "What can you do to solve the problem?" Help people solve their problems, but do not make them yours.

An elementary principal reported how she learned this lesson the hard way: "I took on a lot of the problems of the staff. I wanted to be compassionate . . . I wanted teachers to bring their problems to me. I gave advice, went to their house, took them to dinner. They called me at home. Eventually, I didn't have time for my own family."

Delegate Duties

Some administrators are overworked because they feel indispensable. Certain that nobody could possibly do the job better or do it right, they do everything themselves. Most eventually learn that delegation is essential to survival. One elementary principal said,

Early in my career, I did more schoolwork at home than I did later in my career. Had I continued the pace with which I started, I know I wouldn't have lasted 26 years. I would have burned out long before. I didn't know how to delegate. I really thought that I had to do everything myself. Eventually, I was so overwhelmed that I had to do something. When I couldn't get it all done, I knew that I had to entrust other people with some of the tasks.

One principal said, "Ultimately, you are responsible, but you select the right people for key areas, where they're good at it, and then let them do their job."

Share Leadership

Abundant and varied expertise exists within a group of educators. The wise administrator encourages personnel to assume leadership in areas of expertise. The workload is thereby shared, personnel are invested in school outcomes, and the institution is enriched. Teamwork and building leadership among faculty add to a sense of school ownership. As one high school principal said, "I think it's important to empower teachers to assume some leadership. They are intelligent, capable people. Let them share their talents."

An elementary principal reported, "I'm amazed that some principals won't leave their buildings for fear that something will happen. I put someone capable in charge and leave. If you can't trust the place to run in your absence, something is wrong."

Another high school administrator extolled the use of teamwork: "I formed a leadership team of key personnel who possess varied talents and expertise. When I have a problem, I bring them together and gather their input. Their information, ideas, and suggestions help me make a more informed decision in a shorter period of time."

ONE BITE AT A TIME

How do you eat an elephant? One bite at a time.

—Anonymous

Monumental jobs are completed one small bite at a time. When a huge project looms, break it into smaller parts, each with its own timeline and deadline. One elementary administrator made this comparison: "I complete large projects at work the same way I completed a doctorate—one small chunk at a time. If you worry about the enormity of a job, you'll never get started. Make a plan, focus on the task at hand, check it off, and move to the next."

One Thing at a Time

Some administrators try to do multiple tasks simultaneously—eat lunch, talk on the phone, write a report, and monitor traffic in the outer office. No wonder they feel overwhelmed.

Do one thing at a time. Relax over lunch. Have the phone conversation. Write the report. Close the office door if you are distracted.

Climbing Out of the Pit

Relentless demands and mounting work without a sense of completion are overwhelming. One person compared it to "falling into a bottomless pit. When I finally escape at the end of the day, I'm exhausted and frustrated. There's a mountain of unfinished work on my desk. Tomorrow it will still be there—compounded by whatever new problems the day brings." A high school principal concurred: "When you try to accomplish all the things that need to be done and look at an eight-hour day, it's really a joke."

Despite the demands, some administrators find strategies that bring them a sense of accomplishment and peace of mind. An elementary principal said,

I finish everything on my desk before I leave for the day. Occasionally, I take something home to finish if it requires quiet concentration. I can't enjoy myself until my work is finished. When it's done I forget about work. I relax, and play.

Another elementary principal explained,

I am very organized. I need to have things in order and done in advance. I don't like to do things at the last minute. I don't work well under stress, so I control that by utilizing good time management. I also discovered the need to prioritize and do things that are important . . . and forget about unimportant things.

A high school principal reported,

I try to get everything taken care of during the day. But there are some things that will be a carryover, such as last-minute requests. But the things that need to be done today will be done. The philosophy of trying to handle a piece of paper once is part of what I try to do. By the end of the day, when I clear off my desk, today's priorities will be done. I work about 13 hours a day and sometimes use Saturday morning as a catch-up day.

An elementary principal explained how she prepared for vacations:

I can't leave the building for winter recess until my desk is clear. I don't like the prospect of returning to unfinished tasks. I can't relax knowing that when I come back in January, this stack of work is waiting for me. There are some things you obviously can't finish, but I want to be at a certain point. Then I can leave with a clear conscience. I use checklists and check things off my calendar until I have them all checked off. Then I can relax—forget about work.

Before I leave for summer vacation, I write my opening letters and have the opening newsletters all prepared. Then I can enjoy summer break. I work very, very hard, 15 to 18 hours a day for a few days, to get it done, but it gives me peace of mind not to think about it all summer. I relax all summer and it's much more pleasant to return in the fall.

Some principals occasionally use a weekend day to catch up, while others refuse to do so. One elementary principal observed, "Many principals go into their office on the weekends to get caught up. That's fine if it works for them, but I think it's important to leave it behind for a while—get away from it. I like to get things done during the week and then I can enjoy the reward of being finished."

One high school principal reported, "I sometimes work 11-hour days, but I never take work home. When I'm home, I'm home. My system is prioritizing and planning, working smarter, not harder." While strategies vary, key elements include prioritizing, focusing on essential tasks, delegating low-priority tasks, completing priorities before leaving for the day, and using home time to relax.

SUMMARY

The pressure of time and the staggering workload for school administrators are apparent. To respond to the overload, you must learn to control your environment through organization and staff training. Establishing priorities and a schedule as well as avoiding procrastination are important steps in managing the workload. Learning to say no may be the single most important skill you can acquire. In the next chapter, we discuss the importance of interpersonal skills.

CHAPTER SEVEN

When You're the Dragon

Learning People Skills

Once a human being has arrived on this earth, commun-
ication is the largest single factor determining what kinds
of relationships he makes with others and what happens
to him in the world about him.

—Virginia Satir (*Peoplemaking*, 1972)

A PEOPLE BUSINESS

School administrators are in a people business. Teachers, staff, students, supervisors, parents, and community members demand time, attention, action, and results. Human contacts, often unscheduled and demanding immediate results, are endless.

Dealing with a continuous stream of people and their problems is exhausting. In fact, some researchers proclaim it the most prevalent cause of administrator stress. One high school administrator said, "I feel like I have a sign over my office door, 'Problems welcomed. Come one, come all.'" Another elementary principal said, "A good day is when no parents are waiting for me in the parking lot."

Poor People Skills Lose Jobs

People working in a people business need effective interpersonal skills. Not having them is job threatening. Administrators seldom lose their jobs because of a lack of knowledge. The demise of superintendents stems from political and governance issues and an inability to manage conflict (Bryant & Grady, 1989, 1992; Domenech, 1996; Grady, 1994; Grady & Bryant, 1988, 1990, 1991a, 1991b; McKay & Grady, 1994). The demise of principals arises from the same issues, within the narrower boundaries of the school walls.

Interpersonal Skills Are Critical

Interpersonal skills, however, can be improved. Successful principals have acquired and employ strategies and skills that improve interpersonal relations.

Experience is a great teacher when learning to deal with people. In fact, administrators with less experience tend to experience greater amounts of burnout than do more experienced principals (Carruth, 1997).

As one elementary principal said, "Common sense is an essential part of this job." Acquisition of strategies for working with people, handling problems, resolving conflicts, and communicating enhances job experience. Following are suggestions offered by administrators:

- Interrupt the flow
- Rely on personal power
- Trust people
- Do not overreact to problems
- Put emotions in perspective
- Act on facts—not emotions
- Be direct
- Accept responsibility for your decisions
- Keep your promises.
- Become an expert communicator
- Learn to defuse angry people
- Become an expert in resolving conflicts
- Use common sense

Interrupt the Flow

Endless streams of disagreement, conflicts, and problems are taxing and produce stress. Save your sanity by sandwiching human contact time between tasks that do not involve people. Surround meetings with angry parents with quiet solitude or paperwork. A high school principal commented, "Over the years, I've learned to enjoy solving problems. It gives me a sense of satisfaction to wrestle with a dilemma and resolve it. Of course, there needs to be a limit, a balance in the number of problems."

PERSONAL POWER

Leaders need to be innovators, challengers and energizers of people—administrators who can collaborate and generate high-level performance from personnel. Instead of being sole decision makers, they must become comfortable making collaborative decisions. One elementary principal (whose school has low teacher turnover) said,

> Personal relationships are very important to me. How people feel at work is important. I want them to be comfortable with me and think of me not as a boss, necessarily, but as a colleague. I make the decisions when I need to, but if possible, I prefer collaborative decisions. I enjoy and care about the people who work here. When I do leave, I will miss them terribly.

Principals who interact well with people demonstrate a management style that relies on personal rather than position power. Their interpersonal skills provide strong social support and reduce stress. Principals who rely on position power encounter more stress and higher incidence of burnout (Carruth, 1997). Regardless of style preference, interpersonal skills are a requirement for effective leadership.

Approach People With Trust

Individuals who have a basic trust in people tend to experience fewer conflicts because they frame situations differently

(Covey, 1989). Faced with people of differing viewpoints, one administrator may perceive trouble, while another administrator may perceive innovation. An administrator's approach to people creates potential allies or potential adversaries.

Do Not Overreact

Not every problem demands an immediate solution. Do not overreact when problems erupt. Good decisions require time for gathering information and considering possibilities. Postpone delivering a decision until you can make an informed decision.

Own the Problem

Not all problems belong to you. Do not accept responsibility for the behavior and problems of others. If it is not your problem, return it to the owner. Rather than solving problems for others, teach them problem-solving strategies. One high school principal explained, "Somebody is always coming in and talking to me about their concerns and issues. . . . I find that fun—to talk through problems with people. It's easy for them to solve their own problems, come to their own conclusions by just sharing them."

Put Emotions in Perspective

Administrators are often the brunt of peoples' anger. Regardless of the issue or its source, as the representative of the school, the administrator is charged with the crime and is expected to fix the problem.

It is important to put anger into proper perspective. Although people may target their anger at you, you cannot be responsible for making everything right for everybody. You cannot and will not be able to make everybody happy.

Act on Facts

Consider other people's problems on the basis of factual merits and implications, unclouded by emotions. When the same individual shows up for the third time in a week making false accusations, it is natural to feel anger, hurt, and frustration.

However, acting on those emotions diminishes decisions. One high school principal acknowledged, "My performance was diminished early in my career when I allowed myself to become angry at people."

Sometimes administrators do feel anger, sadness, frustration, and hurt. One elementary principal said, "My feelings are easily hurt. That's a problem for me." These feelings cannot and should not be denied. They exist and need to be expressed, but not during a confrontation with another person. Wait for an appropriate time to express and release them. Sharing the feelings with an understanding colleague helps. As one elementary principal said, "You really can't tell a lot of people how you feel, because unless they've shared the same experiences, they don't understand."

Be Direct

If you are having problems with someone, talk to them. Say, "Let's talk. We need to work this situation out." Avoiding the problem or discussing the problem with other people only makes a bad situation worse. Occasionally, a person assumes that a problem exists when there may be none. Unless people speak directly, small misunderstandings become major problems.

Accept Responsibility for Your Decisions

Accept responsibility for your behavior and your decisions. Be honest. If you do not know the answer to a question, say so. If you make a mistake, acknowledge it. Apologize when necessary. People will value your honesty and sincerity.

DEVELOP COMMUNICATION SKILLS

Open and direct communication is the core of an effective organization. An organization displays dysfunction when it uses indirect forms of communication—people fail to discuss problems openly with the person concerned, preferring to carry tales to others. Or a system of triangulation is used. The principal tells the vice-principal to deliver a message, rather than speaking directly to the person concerned. Written memos, rather than face-to-face meetings, are also symptoms of dysfunction. Gossip and secrets abound. Communications are used to obscure rather than to address problems. Feelings are ignored (Schaef & Fassel, 1988).

The person responsible for establishing effective communication in a school is the principal. Principals need excellent communication skills, because they are at the center of effective interpersonal relations.

A principal's ability to communicate and interact with people reduces and prevents stress for everyone in the building. Principals who spend time smiling, talking, and laughing, and who provide genuine and frequent praise, create positive climates. As one teacher suggested, "Smile. Call us by name. Be friendly. Laugh. Praise genuinely and often."

Conflicts can often be traced to inadequate or ineffective communication skills.

Basic communication skills include

- Active listening
- Giving and receiving appropriate feedback
- Nonverbal communication
- Gender-related speech
- Awareness of cultural diversity
- Conflict resolution skills

Active Listening

When you listen to someone, you tell them that they are worth your time and attention. Failure to listen accounts for many conflicts—in private as well as in professional life. Good listening involves

- Stopping what you are doing
- Clearing away distractions
- Looking at the person
- Not interrupting
- Focusing on what is being said
- Keeping an open mind
- Asking questions to clarify your understanding
- Listening between the lines for values and feelings

Giving Feedback

Administrators frequently give and receive feedback. Formal teacher evaluations and informal classroom observations are familiar school routines. Of particular importance is letting others know when they are doing a good job.

Giving negative feedback creates potentially tense situations for teachers and administrators. Suggestions for delivering negative feedback include

- Delivering feedback privately, without anger or personal attack. If necessary, wait until your anger subsides before speaking with the person.
- Reporting observable findings without judgment, accusations, or interpretations of motive: "I have observed that your students were left alone in the classroom three times this week," instead of, "You're irresponsible—leaving students alone all the time."
- Be clear. Identify the objectionable behavior: "You have left your students unattended and unsupervised three times this week. During one of those occasions, a student was injured. You may not leave students unattended at any time."
- Explain your concern: "I am concerned that students are losing instructional time, and I am also worried about serious student injury occurring."
- Specify the changes you want to occur: "I want you to be in the classroom at all times. If you must leave, contact the office for assistance."
- State the possible consequences: "If your behavior changes immediately, we won't mention this again. However, if it continues, this issue will be part of your personnel evaluation. In addition, you run the risk of a lawsuit if a student is injured."
- Invite the individual to respond. Although the need for proper behavior will not change, the individual may need your guidance in addressing intervening personal issues: "I've been leaving the room because I've been getting sick during the day" or "I'm leaving the room to call the hospital. My husband is very ill and I'm worried."
- If the situation warrants it, set an appointment for a follow-up meeting.
- Document the meeting.

Receiving Feedback

Principals receive constant feedback, often negative, from parents, teachers, and supervisors. Knowing how to handle the information can make the situation more comfortable and the information more useful. DuBrin (1997) offers the following:

- Do not become defensive. Detach yourself emotionally and just listen.
- Consider the credibility and knowledge level of the information source.
- Ask for clarification and specifics regarding the criticism.
- Respond appropriately. Let the critic know on what issues you agree. If you disagree, thank the person for the information. Openly disagreeing aggravates the situation. If you realize you are at fault, apologize.
- Disarm the critic by asking how you can improve the situation: "What would you like to see happen?"

Nonverbal Communication

Trite but true, "Actions speak louder than words." When verbal and nonverbal messages are inconsistent, the nonverbal message is the one believed. A classic study by Albert Mehrabian revealed that 93% of communication is nonverbal (DuBrin, 1997). Here are some suggestions to consider:

Eye Contact. Looking at people when you speak to them shows respect. Eye contact indicates interest, while avoidance indicates the opposite.

Posture. Match posture to the message you want to convey. Posture provides clues to how you feel. Your choice of posture expresses confidence, enthusiasm, and relaxation, or tension and displeasure.

Facial Expressions. Control facial expressions. People are quick to sense a contradiction between what you say and the expression you wear.

Voice Quality. How you sound is more important than what you say. The emotions behind the voice deliver a strong message.

Interpersonal Distance. Be aware of your use of space. More space is more formal; less is intimate. If you remain behind your desk, you appear unapproachable. If you sit next to a person, you appear welcoming.

Appearance. Choice of clothing and grooming are powerful messages. People tend to respond positively to people who are well dressed but not overdressed.

Environment. The setting in which a message is transmitted affects its importance. Temperature, lighting, furniture arrangement, and neatness of the room also relay nonverbal messages.

Diversity of Cultures

Schools are becoming more culturally diverse. Behaviors of members of the school community may vary according to ethnic origin. Problems can be avoided by knowing the norms of the cultures within the school. Differences include (a) the importance of individualism versus collectivism, (b) body language, such as proximity and eye contact, (c) child-rearing practices, (d) time orientation, and (e) importance of materialism versus concern for others.

One elementary administrator recalled an incident that revealed the need to understand students' cultures: "A furious teacher brought a young man to my office, complaining of his disrespectfulness. 'He won't look at me when I speak to him,' she complained. I pointed out that the student was Native American and the behavior that she requested was considered to be impolite by Native Americans."

Gender

Misunderstandings occur between genders when men and women misinterpret the motivation of each other's communications. Men and women possess different preferences in communication styles. While individual preferences are more important than stereotypes, awareness of differences in communication patterns can eliminate communication barriers.

Women use conversation to build rapport with others. When they have a problem, they use conversation to gain empathy and support. Their focus on relationship building prompts them to be conciliatory in the face of differences. They tend to be polite and complimentary to others.

Men use talk to display their knowledge and skills. They are directive in conversations, prefer to work out their problems alone, and are comfortable calling attention to their accomplishments. They tend to dominate discussions during meetings.

Understanding gender differences in communication promotes more accurate interpretations of the behavior and communications of coworkers.

CONFLICT

Conflict, although unwelcome, is part of the normal functioning of an organization. In fact, the exchange of ideas during conflict resolution can serve a functional purpose. Conflict that focuses on ideas is positive, while conflict that focuses on personalities is destructive.

Malicious Conflict

Conflict becomes malicious when people are attacked or when the aggressor acts out of malice with the intention to harm either an individual or an organization. One principal described an example of angry parents with malicious intentions:

> I had two racist families who had been forced to participate in the school's desegregation plan. They were furious and reminded me of that at least twice a week when they came in unannounced and told me tales of the African American students threatening white students with knives. Then they'd call the television stations, and I literally had reporters hiding behind the bushes to see if they could get a story. They went to every school board meeting with horrific stories about me, the school, teachers, and neighborhood. Of course, none of the stories were true, but they made it a dreadful year. I was close to burnout—ready to throw in the towel.

Sources of Conflict

Conflict emerges from three sources: (1) parties have incompatible goals, (2) parties want different solutions, but only one is possible, and (3) parties want the same thing, but only one can have it. The main source of conflict in schools is adults: parent to teacher and teacher to teacher (Payne, 1994).

The principals we interviewed concurred. "The students aren't the problem. It's the adults—complaining parents and difficult teachers." These conflicts pose difficult situations because preservation of the relationships is essential.

Angry Confrontations

Administrators understandably dread confrontations with angry individuals. Sooner or later, most administrators experience an angry person shouting either at them or a school employee.

Anger, defensiveness, and fear are natural feelings under these conditions. Typical responses to anger include ignoring, ridiculing, walking away, or counterattacking. However, these responses may escalate the anger and the potential for violence.

Instead, concentrate on diffusing the individual's emotions. Never underestimate the potential for violence from an angry person. Train office staff to alert security personnel whenever someone appears to be emotionally out of control. All staff should know crisis procedures and feel free to enact them at the hint of any potential danger. Keep students out of the area.

Counter strong emotions with a polite, calm manner. Greet the individual and introduce yourself. Speak slowly and quietly, indicating that you would like to hear the problem. Guide the person to a location where your conversation will not disturb others—but within view of office personnel who can monitor the situation. Invite the person to sit down. Seat yourself near the door, with a table or desk between you and out of arm's reach of the individual. Assure the individual that you are concerned, interested, and willing to listen. Insist, however, on a conversational tone and no offensive language. Offer the person something to drink. Your goal is to enable the individual to regain composure.

If the person is willing to tell you the problem in a civil manner, listen without interrupting. Listen for the emotions to dissipate. Then restate the problem to verify your understanding of the information and feelings presented. Do not argue, even if you disagree. Once a mutual understanding of the problem has been reached, assure the individual that you will look into the situation. Before ending the meeting, set an appointment to discuss a solution. Try to end the meeting on a cordial tone—with a smile and handshake.

If the individual becomes verbally abusive or threatening, end the meeting, tell the person to leave the building, and exit the room. Obtain security or law enforcement assistance if necessary.

A high school principal described his strategies:

> I don't like conflicts, never seek them out, but I don't back away either. I've learned how to deal with them. When people call or come in with a burr under their saddle, I've learned to let them talk it out, to listen, yet let them know that I'm in charge. But I also make sure that I'm well prepared with the facts before we meet again to discuss the problem.

Resolving Conflicts

In a conflict, individuals may be upset and frustrated. Time and good listening skills are necessary to release emotions before engaging in problem-solving strategies.

The process of dealing with conflict generally includes

- Listening to the person describe the problem. Pay attention to feelings and beliefs, as well as facts. Encourage their version without interjecting your opinions. When they finish, ask questions for clarification. Then restate the problem as you heard it: "This is what I heard you say . . ." Listen for agreement. When you both agree on the problem, move to the next step.
- Stating your perception of the problem. Say, "Now that I understand your concerns, I'll share my perceptions. You may not agree, but when I finish, we will examine where we agree and where we disagree." Tell your version. Be prepared for opposition. When you finish, try to get the individual to repeat your version to clarify understanding.
- Determining if a problem remains. When people share perceptions, misunderstandings are clarified and problems sometimes vanish. State the problem as simply as possible. Determine the points where you agree and the points where you disagree.
- If a solution is negotiable, generating solutions to solve the problem. If a solution is not negotiable, tell the person so.

- Selecting a solution that serves the interests of both parties. If the decision is yours, convey your decision and rationale to the individual. When the issues concern personal beliefs or school policies, sometimes the only solution is agreeably agreeing to disagree.
- If needed, developing an action plan to implement the solution.
- Evaluating the process.

Communication skills are learned and, like all skills, require practice.

SUMMARY

Successful principals acquire and employ strategies and skills that improve interpersonal relations. Leaders need to be innovators, challengers, and energizers of people—administrators who can collaborate and generate high-level performance from personnel. A principal's ability to communicate and interact with people reduces and prevents stress for everyone in the building. Leaders who spend time smiling, talking, and laughing and who provide genuine and frequent praise create positive climates. The next chapter focuses on professional renewal.

CHAPTER EIGHT

Changing Dragons

Career Renewal

What is death to the caterpillar to the butterfly is being set free.

—Anonymous

CAREER STRESS

Administrators exhibit career stress in a variety of ways. Some dread going to work, dislike their jobs, and live for the day they can retire. Others suffer exhaustion, exhibit physical symptoms of excess stress, are bored, would like a change, but feel they have no career alternatives.

Frustrated principals describe their reasons for leaving the principalship as increasing job demands, lack of role clarity, lack of recognition, and decreasing autonomy due to collaborative decision making (Whitaker, 1995).

Too much stress and too little stress affect job satisfaction and performance. A certain amount of stress is necessary for motivation and challenge, but too much stress contributes to burnout and illness. In the eye of a hurricane, a brilliant flame is soon extinguished.

Too Much Stress

I would rather that my spark should burn out in a brilliant blaze than it should be stifled by dry rot.

—Jack London

A certain amount of stress motivates peak performance; too much stress causes talented administrators to burn out.

Administrators have experienced profound changes in job requirements and increased dependence on technology. Computers, fax machines, and voice mail have become integral to daily life. Administrators are constantly updating their technology skills.

Some administrators welcome the changes, but other administrators are frustrated by or resistant to change. One elementary principal, pointing to a new computer on her desk, said, "The school is full of computers, the library card catalog is computerized, and I don't know how to use that computer on my desk." Another said, "I hate e-mail. I just can't get used to using it."

Too Little Stress

Rather than being overstressed, some administrators are understimulated. These administrators may have selected the wrong career or accepted the wrong position. Not everyone is suited to be an administrator, and not everyone is suited to every school setting. One principal said, "I was happy and successful for 10 years at my first school. But I was plagued with problems with parents at the next one. The stress was unbearable." Boredom can also result from staying in one place too long. When the challenge is gone, it's time to move on. As one principal pointed out, "I knew it was time to leave when it wasn't exciting to come to work anymore."

The perception of too much or too little stress is an individual matter. A cause for stress for one administrator may be regarded as a challenge by another.

Common causes of stress-related problems include

- Lack of professional development
- Remaining too long in one position

- Mismatch in position
- Unsuitable career choice
- Life-cycle transitions

PROFESSIONAL RENEWAL

School administration has moved in new directions. Clients have changed, and technologies have expanded. School leaders must be able to work collaboratively, develop shared visions, and challenge people to new levels. Administrators require skills that enable them to facilitate group processes.

Administrators whose professional growth lags behind current developments need retooling to meet the expectations of their jobs. Having the skills to do their job well is essential to reducing stress.

Directing Your Own Renewal

Some school districts fail to address the professional development needs of administrators or expect them to participate in teachers' programs. One high school administrator said, "I had excellent staff development at one of my locations and absolutely nothing geared toward administrators at the last setting."

Administrators must take responsibility for their professional growth and renewal, because the most effective professional growth is self-initiated and self-directed. The best incentive for lasting change is personal desire, not direction from an outside source.

A professional development plan includes the following steps:

- Setting objectives
- Creating an action plan
- Specifying activities
- Establishing target dates
- Determining a method to obtain feedback

Sources of Professional Renewal

Administrators use the following methods of renewal:

- Attending professional conferences
- Reading professional journals and books

- Networking with colleagues
- Attending workshops
- Teaching college courses
- Engaging in research
- Writing for publication
- Presenting at conferences
- Engaging in graduate study
- Visiting other educational systems
- Creating a new program
- Mentoring new administrators

Administrators reported the following activities:

I attend professional meetings. I wish I could tell you that I read all sorts of professional things that provide wonderful ideas, but it isn't easy to find time for reading. I skim through an education newspaper once a week and see if there's anything I want to follow up on.

I enjoy . . . opportunities to visit with colleagues from all over the country. Some of the best discussions occur at conferences, standing around with a doughnut and a cup of coffee, talking to somebody from another state. To be able to do that more intensely in a retreat setting would be just great.

I teach summer school courses at the university. It keeps me on the cutting edge of my field, and the interaction with students and professors is intellectually stimulating.

Teaching college courses takes me into a world of learning that's entirely different from my work at school. The students' energy energizes me. I feel better after class than I do after working all day at school.

Preparing staff development programs for my teachers is a stimulating experience, similar to that of college teaching.

Sometimes I present at administrator conferences. I learn a lot by sharing what I'm doing at my school and obtaining feedback from colleagues.

I mentor others who are entering the profession.

REVISING A CAREER

If in the last few years you haven't discarded a major opinion or acquired a new one, check your pulse, you may be dead.

—Gelett Burgess

Unfortunately, individuals develop ruts in their behavior that are tenacious. School administrators become stuck in ruts of their own making. They may be unhappy or bored with their current job. We cannot expect constant job satisfaction and fulfillment. However, if despite renewal efforts you experience prolonged boredom, dissatisfaction, or burnout, it may be time to revise your career plans.

Staying Too Long in One Place

Many administrators enjoy years of success in one position. They enjoy being innovators and risk takers, updating their job skills, and working at their profession. However, for others, staying too long in one position may be a source of boredom and career dissatisfaction.

The number of years of experience administrators have and how long they hold a position are related to burnout. Individuals with more experience tend to suffer less burnout if their experience is not limited to one position (Linthicum, 1994, as cited in Carruth, 1997). The stimulation of different positions produces a positive effect and decreases the probability of burnout. Changing schools or districts can provide the stimulation and challenge to reenergize a career.

Administrators revealed that they knew it was time to move on "when you become too comfortable and the excitement is gone," "when I felt like I owned the school," "when I had finished what I wanted to do. It was time for somebody else to add the next layer—new ideas."

Changing Schools

Many years ago, workers in the coal mines of Pennsylvania took canaries into the mines. As long as the canary was singing, workers knew that the air was safe to breathe. When the canary stopped singing, they knew the workplace was toxic and it was time to leave.

—P. Barrentine (1993)

School leaders can find themselves in the wrong settings. Sometimes good administrators are miserable because they are mismatched with the school or the community. One high school administrator said,

I'm amazed that my career has worked out as well as it did, because in my earlier years, I didn't plan well. I changed jobs whenever I saw a better opportunity, meaning higher pay and more prestige. Now I'm more analytical in looking for a position that matches my style and my skills.

An elementary principal said,

It's tremendously important to match a school community to an administrator. While I haven't been in a bad situation, in three out of the four schools I've served, there was a better match in three of them. It's very important to match a person's aptitudes with the needs of the community.

Sometimes administrators make poor choices and find themselves in destructive situations. One elementary principal reported leaving her job because "I was, in essence, being emotionally and professionally abused."

Revising Your Role

Too many years in an administrative role could lead to boredom and lack of stimulation. Often administrators can be reenergized by new roles. Administrators reported,

I've discovered that I enjoy college teaching much more than I do administration. I'm looking forward to a career change to the university.

I'm ready for the new challenges of a central office position. The prospect of using my expertise in curriculum is exciting.

I'm looking for a change. I'm tired of being a principal. The role, the tasks, are no longer challenging and exciting. It has nothing to do with my present job situation; I'm just ready for the next stage of my development.

CHANGING CAREERS

Dear Dorothy: Hate Oz, took the shoes, find your own way home. –Toto.

—Anonymous

Some administrators are following someone else's path. They spend their lives following goals that they did not select for themselves. Increasingly unhappy and dissatisfied, they dread going to work.

People end up in the wrong careers for many reasons. The mismatch may be due to the influence of well-meaning parents, spouses, friends, mentors, and college advisers.

Inexperience is another factor. It is difficult to know if a career is a match unless you try it. Some administrators discover on the job that their personalities are not suited for the tasks of administration. Not all individuals find dealing with criticism, interruptions, fragmented work, and occasional crises as satisfying work.

Individuals may outgrow a career. As adults continue to grow and develop, so too do their needs and motivations. A high school principal said, "I liked being a principal, but now I'm ready to move on. I no longer find it challenging. I need to change directions."

Given limited opportunities for advancement, some individuals take administrative positions for the wrong reasons, such as more money or status. Regardless of the reason, when work is devoid of satisfaction, it is time to establish new goals and a new path.

The Ties That Bind

Administrators may remain in jobs that no longer fit. Once settled in a career, it is difficult to make a major change. A job may be tolerated with the expectation that it will get better. Alternatives may not be apparent. Individuals have (a) worked hard to establish careers, (b) have families who depend on them, (c) may not know how to do anything else, or (d) may be afraid to change careers. Taylor (1998) described similar dependencies occurring in marriages, prisons, chemical addictions, races, as well as jobs. Given the opportunity for greater happiness, people are afraid to leave their comfort zone to pursue new opportunities.

Organizations are difficult to leave. They have a way of becoming central to our life, providing meaning, social interaction, and rewards. For some individuals, loyalty to the organization becomes a substitute for living their own lives. Gradually, they lose touch with what they feel, know, and believe. Instead of pursuing what they want, they follow the promise of the organization, looking to it for security and a sense of worth (Schaef & Fassel, 1988). The security of financial benefits imposes an additional inhibitor.

Making Sure the Grass Is Greener

Career changes require serious deliberation. We all have days, even weeks, when we feel disheartened, bemoan our fate, dream about a better position, or look enviably at other positions. Erma Bombeck said it best: "The grass is always greener over the septic tank."

Selecting a Course of Action

Examine your past work situations. Consider the times when you were totally engaged in your work, when what you were doing was thoroughly fulfilling and rewarding. Time slipped away while you worked. You experienced a sense of satisfaction and pleasure and looked forward to resuming the task (Grensing-Pophal, 1999). What were you doing? How does what you are doing today compare to that activity?

Taking a Sabbatical

You don't realize the stress you're under until you're no longer under it.

—A high school principal

Taking a sabbatical, if possible, is an excellent choice for someone considering a significant career change. Vacations provide short-term, reenergizing benefits; however, a sabbatical provides an opportunity to acquire new perspectives and consider the pros and cons of a change. An examination of the satisfying and unsatisfying aspects of a job is possible when we are free of daily routines. A sabbatical may reenergize a return to a previous job or facilitate a change to a new one.

Life Transitions

Timing Career Moves

School administration may be the perfect career choice. However, timing the move to administration plays a critical role in your success. Personal circumstances are important considerations. New marriages, pregnancies, dual careers, and parenting young children are time consuming and stress producing. The added responsibilities of school administration may not be the best choice under these circumstances.

Although some young couples successfully cope with pregnancy, parenting, and dual careers, stress takes a toll. Marriages and careers can be jeopardized. As one administrator explained, "I delayed becoming a principal until my children were older. With both of our careers, we couldn't have handled our job responsibilities and taken proper care of our children."

Know when to hold 'em, know when to fold 'em.

—Johnny Cash

Retiring

Not unlike a game of poker, school leaders need to recognize when it is time to quit. Some individuals are ready to retire early in life, while others happily and productively continue into advanced age. Much depends on their health situation as well as personal needs and desires. The key is knowing when the time is right.

Regardless of when you decide to leave, it is best to leave while holding a hand of aces. Retiring when things are going well enables you to leave with a sense of satisfaction. Remaining too long risks diminished productivity. Upon entering her 70s, one school leader instructed her supervisor,

> I don't want to become an educator who ceases to be progressive and productive, the one that everyone wishes would go away. Promise me that if I fail to see it happening, you will tell me that it's time to retire.

Health Issues

Regardless of age, retirement or disability should be considered when your health begins to diminish. Although it is difficult to leave a fulfilling career, the long-term effects of both personal health and job performance must be considerations. Making a graceful exit while you are still satisfied with your performance is the better choice.

SUMMARY

Administrators must take responsibility for their professional growth and renewal, because the most effective professional growth is self-initiated and self-directed. For some individuals, changing schools or roles can be energizing. As part of professional development, it is important to consider your career path and possible alternative paths. Review, revision, and recommitment are important steps in career examination and reflection. The subject of the next chapter is taking care of yourself.

CHAPTER NINE

Making Friends With the Dragon

Taking Care of Yourself

*I was born to catch dragons in their dens and pick
flowers.*

—James Kavanaugh

REALIZING YOUR IMPORTANCE

School leaders are engaged in the critical role of educating the
youth who will catapult the world into the future. As Goodman
(1998) observed, "Principals have been given the point position in
the illusive quest for the 'effective' school, and accountability
for success or failure has been laid directly on their shoulders,
even though they have little control over an external definition of
effectiveness" (p. 1).

Although society may not recognize or reward the efforts of
school leaders, the future depends on their effectiveness. Personal
effectiveness, however, depends on maintaining an intellectual
edge while sustaining enthusiasm and stamina in the face of a
challenging job.

Reflecting on Others

School leaders must be conscious of how their responses to stress affect others. Principals establish the emotional tone in their work settings. Whatever behaviors they notice, reward, and practice are adopted as school norms. Some leaders create emotionally supportive climates; others create emotionally stressful ones.

Despite frustrations and hassles, many principals find ways to maintain their energy, commitment, and motivation. Their actions motivate and energize their subordinates and colleagues. Other principals allow stress to control their actions. A principal who is a workaholic encourages teachers to value and practice workaholic behavior. A leader who displays stress-filled behaviors creates a stress-filled school environment with high incidence of teacher burnout. Burnout is contagious (Brock & Grady, 2000).

Finding Your Balance

The demands of school leadership simultaneously require and threaten mental and physical health and stamina. The pace, uncertainty, ambiguity, and conflict involved in the job make school administrators candidates for stress. Eight-hour days and 40-hour weeks do not exist in their fast-paced world.

Stress is integral to the job, but it must not be taken for granted. Each individual's capacity for stress is limited. When the limits are exceeded, the individual is susceptible to disease. Despite this, most administrators behave as though they have an unlimited capacity for stress. They take on projects, commitments, and burdens and seldom consider the consequences to their mental and physical well-being. They tend to deny the extent of their stress, ignoring its physical signs while wondering why their personal relationships are faltering.

Long-term stress is seductive and numbing. Once engaged in a job, we become habituated to it and we lose perspective.

Danger signals include the following:

- Work, previously satisfying, is becoming a stressful obsession.
- Work is taking precedence over self-care.
- Work is becoming an external referent for self-worth.

CARING FOR YOURSELF

People who want your time and abilities do not worry about the consequences to your health and personal life. If you allow them to consume you, only you will pay the consequences.

Although you are an educator, manager, and leader, you are more than any one of these roles. At your center is your inner person, determined by your character, values, beliefs, commitments, and internal balance. Your inner person is the store of inner strength that sustains you. Keeping physically and emotionally fit, reflecting on practice, and growing professionally are means to nurture the inner self (Speck, 1999).

One means of becoming acquainted with your inner person is through reflective thinking, a means of examining your motives and actions. Thinking reflectively requires honesty. Done regularly, it enables you to maintain perspective and direction and serves as a guide for personal and professional development. Accept the reality of limitations and embrace the possibilities in your life (see Resource B).

Finding Your Comfort Level

We always work a little better when there's a little anxiety, a little stress to keep us on the edge.

—A high school principal

Stress is internally created when we interpret and assign power to an event. How much power we assign determines the level of stress we experience.

You have the power to control your response to stress and use it to your advantage.

Examining Motivation

Stress is a product of your way of thinking. Who you are, what you believe, and what motivates you is acted out in every decision and action. Central to changing behavior is changing the way you think and what prompts your actions.

People do things that bring satisfaction. Some folks are happy selling flower leis along Hawaiian roadsides. Others require the thrill of conquest, even danger. A few persevere over a lifetime to attain excellence in their field. Most of us are somewhere in the middle. Determining and fulfilling personal motivation is the basis of happiness.

What needs motivate your actions? Is it

- Power
- Money
- Recognition
- Satisfaction
- Security
- Status
- Love
- Risk
- Adventure

CHANGING RESPONSES

A new philosophy, a way of life, is not given for nothing. It has to be paid dearly for and only acquired with much patience and great effort.

—Fyodor Dostoyevsky

If everyone who read self-help books followed their advice, the population of the United States would be slim, healthy, and relaxed. Yet the citizenry continues to be overweight, out of shape, and frazzled. Despite knowledge and motivation, our efforts to change our behavior are often short lived. Old behaviors quickly reappear.

Old habits are strong and jealous.

—Dorothea Brande

The culprit is habit. Long-term behaviors become deeply ingrained habits that are difficult to change. Pavlov's conditioning is at work when an individual who is experiencing stress returns to the substance that brought relief. While the rational mind wants a change, the subconscious mind struggles tenaciously to maintain a familiar, comfortable behavior. Knowing what behaviors need changing and effecting a lasting change are two different things. Something is required to bridge the gap between knowledge and application.

Replacing Bad Habits With Good Ones

If you don't like something, change it. If you can't change it,
change your attitude. Don't complain.

—Maya Angelou

Undesirable behaviors and habits usually arise as temporary or quick solutions for unmet needs, many of which are triggered by stress. The habits serve as distractions and temporary comfort from a larger problem, such as criticism, rejection, or feelings of inadequacy. As one elementary principal acknowledged, "I tend to overeat when I'm under stress." While the problem at work may still need to be resolved, identifying and correcting an inappropriate coping response is a beginning.

Make a list of the issues that cause you stress and your undesirable coping responses. This is an important step in raising the awareness necessary for change. Be sure these are habits you want to change. Changing behavior to please someone else is seldom effective. Only you can change your behavior.

Identify alternatives to the undesirable habits. Motivation for lasting change is limited unless a positive substitution fills the gap.

Once you have made your list of bad habits and replacement habits, select only one habit to work on at a time. Attempting too many changes at once will have an outcome similar to last year's New Year's resolutions. Do not expect instant miracles. Changing habits takes time, practice, and persistence.

Principals who are skilled in conflict resolution are aware of the benefits of these skills. Yet, knowing the skills and becoming accustomed to using them are entirely different. One principal said, "Learning to listen to an angry parent without interrupting was difficult. I felt the need to interrupt to defend myself or the teacher, as though my listening would be interpreted as agreement." Her dilemma was relieved only by practice. Once she felt comfortable with the new behavior and experienced positive results, the behavior became part of her repertoire.

Expect some relapses into old behavior, and when they occur, forgive yourself and begin again. Repetition is what creates habits, good ones and bad ones. Although at first the new behavior may seem unnatural, practice will make it routine. Eventually, your habits can serve rather than control you. See Resource C for a worksheet for personal change. Resource D provides a model for change.

Picking Flowers

This book is not a substitute for recognition, higher salaries, trips to Hawaii, or other well-deserved stress relievers, but rather it is a tool to catch and tame the dragons that dominate administrators' lives and threaten success. If administrators are to flourish, they must recognize and corral the destructiveness of personal stress. Although you may not be able to change all the stressors in your life, you can change some of them and change how you relate to the others.

As with most complex dilemmas, there are solutions but not quick fixes or easy answers. Each administrator's dragon is unique, requiring personal innovation in its capture and taming. Central to the solution, however, is taking action. Knowledge must translate to application and practice for the benefit to occur.

Some administrators will read this book and promise themselves that "one day I'll do something about my stress problem." Of course, "one day" seldom arrives, and they remain mired in a rut, while the dragon enjoys free reign over their lives.

Other administrators will use this book to catch the dragon by its tail, make positive lifestyle changes, and spend more time in the activities they enjoy, possibly picking flowers. We hope you are one of them.

SUMMARY

As a school leader, you must find ways to maintain your energy, commitment, and motivation. You have the power to control your response to stress and use it to your advantage!

Responses to Stress

DESTRUCTIVE RESPONSES TO STRESS

- Sugar, easily absorbed into the bloodstream, raises short-term energy. The body copes by secreting insulin to reduce the sugar levels, which causes an energy dip.

- Caffeine, found in coffee, chocolate, soda, and tea, gives an energizing boost, one that actually increases stress.

- Alcohol helps people feel energized and aggressive, diminishes sensation, and increases pleasure.

- Nicotine is an extremely toxic chemical that increases the heart rate while giving the smoker a short-term feeling of relaxation.

- Prescription pills give quick fixes that ignore underlying causes of stress and can cause dependency.

- Adrenaline produces a high from risky behaviors, such as dangerous sports or gambling. Workaholics and shopaholics fall into this category, as they use their own adrenaline to keep stimulated.

- Yelling and allowing feelings to build until emotional control is lost result in damaged relationships.

- Fighting and loss of emotional control are behaviors that create rather than solve problems.

- Complaining and seeking sympathy do not enhance the professional work environment.

- Sulking, self-pity, and behaving as a victim are destructive behaviors that are inappropriate to professional settings.

- Worry wastes time and energy, and often the anticipated crisis never occurs.

POSITIVE RESPONSES TO STRESS

- Alter personal attitudes, perspectives, and behaviors.
- Set personal and professional goals for yourself.
- Develop an internal locus of control.
- Overcome the need for perfection.
- Slow your pace.
- Ignore trivial problems.
- Assign less power to problems.
- Get rid of old grudges.
- Control your emotions.
- Use sound problem-solving strategies.
- Delegate.
- Ask for help when you need it.
- Put worries into perspective.
- Use cognitive restructuring.
- Focus on success.
- Laugh out loud.
- Exercise.

- Maintain good nutrition.
- Rest.
- Get a massage.
- Pray.
- Meditate.
- Practice visualization.
- Use progressive relaxation.
- Develop hobbies.
- Socialize with friends.
- Talk with family.
- Play.
- Include solitude in every day.

Realities and Possibilities

The fault finder will find fault even in Paradise. Love your life.

—Henry David Thoreau

ACCEPT REALITY

- Not everyone will like you.
- Not everyone will appreciate your efforts.
- Not everyone will value your work.
- Not everyone will agree with you.
- You don't own all the problems.
- You can't make the world perfect.
- You can't control how others think or behave.
- You can't control what happens tomorrow.
- You can't change what happened yesterday.
- You can't protect those you love from disappointment or pain.
- You can't do everything for everyone.

- You can't make someone else happy.
- You can't please everybody.
- Love and friendship lost will reappear in someone else.
- Holding a grudge serves no worthwhile purpose.
- Stress occurs when you allow other people and circumstances to dictate how you feel.

EMBRACE POSSIBILITIES

- You can love and allow yourself to be loved.
- You can reward yourself for accomplishments.
- You can believe in the importance of your work.
- You can be open to the ideas of others.
- You can take responsibility for your own problems and behavior.
- You can make the world better by your presence.
- You can choose to look at the future with confidence.
- You can control how you feel, think, and behave today.
- You can choose to be happy or unhappy, stressed or serene.
- You can let go of the past.
- You can change what is changeable.
- You can find your center, your spirit.
- You can surround yourself with positive people.
- You can avoid unacceptable behavior, people, and situations.
- You can live in the moment.
- You can simplify your life.
- You can count your blessings daily.

Stress Reduction

An Outline for Personal Change

If you can change it, change it
If you can't change it, change yourself
If you can't change it and can't live with it, leave

I. The Stress: What situations cause your stress?

    A. List the stressful problems in your personal life.

    B. List the stressful problems in your professional life.

    C. Identify the stressful problems that aren't very important. Cross them off your lists. Focus on what's important.

    D. Identify any stress problems that are part of an old grudge. Cross them off your list and let them go.

II. The Cause: What contributes to your stress? *Some problems may have more than one contributor. If so, indicate all.*

    A. *Personality.* Circle the stressful situations created or extenuated by your personality (e.g., perfectionism, workaholism, competitiveness, or need to overachieve).

B. *Attitude*. Identify stressful situations that you lack power to change but you can reduce by a change in the way you approach them (e.g., your attitude). Draw a box around these.

C. *Skills*. Identify stressful situations caused by lack of skill at work or home (e.g., technology, time management, communication, or parenting). Put a check mark next to these.

D. *Behavior*. Identify stressful situations that can be reduced by a change in your response or behavior. Put an X next to them.

E. *Not changeable*. The stressful situations remaining should be ones that you perceive are unchangeable, e.g., the organizational structure of your district or financial resources. Place an asterisk (*) next to them.

F. Arrange your stressful situations in lists according to sources: personality, attitude, skills, behavior, not changeable, and multiple. Next to each situation, identify an action you can take to relieve it.

III. Solutions: What can you do about it?

A. *Personality*. Examine the stressors you circled as personality issues. What personality trait is causing the problem? How can you change this trait?

B. *Attitude*. Examine the stressors that can be relieved by a change of attitude. What new approach can you take to reduce the stress?

C. *Skills*. What skill deficits are contributing to your stress? How can you learn the skills?

D. *Behavior.* What stress can be reduced by a change in your response or behavior? Identify a behavior change you can make.

E. *Unchangeable*. How serious are the unchangeable problems that cause your stress? Can you live with them, or do you need to leave the work setting? What are your options if you leave?

F. *Multiple sources.* Sometimes stress is the result of multiple sources. For instance, personality trait and behavior: perfectionism coupled with taking on too many tasks at once. Identify options to address each of the sources.

IV. Plan of Action: What will you do?

  A. Determine the best course of action for each problem.
  B. Prioritize your list.
  C. Work on one problem at a time.
  D. Practice the new behavior. Habits are persistent. New behaviors must be practiced until they become part of routine behavior. They will feel uncomfortable at first. Wait until the new behavior or attitude is integrated into your behavior pattern before tackling a response to the next stressor.
  E. Be aware that your change of behavior may receive a negative response from others. For instance, if you have allowed teachers and parents to wander in and interrupt you all day, they may be annoyed when you stop that practice.

V. Periodic Evaluation: Why re-evaluate?

  A. Nothing stays the same. Life, work, problems, and sources of stress change quickly. Periodic evaluation of stress levels, their sources, and revised action plans are necessary.

Corner the dragon in its den one step at a time.

Model Action Plan

I. The Problem: Stress created by workload extending beyond the day

II. Causes

    A. Perfectionism; feeling I need to do everything myself

    B. Taking on too many activities

    C. Too many interruptions

III. Solutions

    A. Perfectionism

        1. Identification of work that can be delegated

        2. Identification of qualified individuals for delegated duties

    B. Taking on too much

        1. Identification of priorities and high-payoff tasks

        2. Saying no to tasks that do not fall within those priorities

C. Interruptions

    1. Closing the office door for a period of time each day

    2. Scheduling appointments

D. Implementation

    1. Delegate work to qualified individuals and allow them to handle it without interference.

    2. Arrange a daily schedule that allows for appointments, time to return telephone calls, and time to work without interruptions—closed door and no calls.

    3. Keep a list of today's priority tasks on the desk. After interruptions, return to the task. When a task is completed, check it off and move to the next task.

    4. List the priorities for your current position and your professional aspirations. If proposed activities will not enhance your professional aspirations or benefit your current position, say no.

    5. Learn to say no gracefully. Practice until you have phrases that feel comfortable.

IV. Consider possible consequences of my new behaviors

A. Problems

    1. Overburdening staff with delegated duties

    2. Selecting the wrong person for a delegated duty

    3. Negative reactions from teachers and parents to a closed door and request for appointments

    4. Negative reactions from colleagues and staff accustomed to you saying yes to additional duties

V. Evaluation

A. Did I delegate important items to qualified staff?

B. Did I allow staff to work without interference?

C. Did I minimize interruptions?

D. Did I accomplish more each day by using the time I saved?

E. Did I eliminate extra work by saying no to low-priority activities?

F. Did I avoid or respond appropriately to negative reactions to my new behaviors?

G. Do I need to change or modify my action plan?

References

Adams, M. (1999). Emily Dickinson had a dog: An interpretation of the human-dog bond. *Anthrozoos, 12*(3), 132-137.

Amundson, K. (1993). *Keeping spirits high.* Arlington, VA: American Association of School Administrators.

Aneshensel, C. S., & Pearlin, L. I. (1987). Structural contexts of sex differences in stress. In R. C. Barnett, L. Biener, & G. K. Baruch (Eds.), *Gender and stress* (pp. 75-95). New York: Free Press.

Barrentine, P. (Ed.). (1993). *When the canary stops singing.* San Francisco: Berrett-Koehler.

Brady, E. J. (1989). The relationship of locus of control, perceived leadership styles, and job satisfaction of supervisors. (Doctoral dissertation, Mississippi State University). *Dissertation Abstracts International, 49* (12-B, Pt 1), 5555.

Brock, B. L., & Fraser, J. (2001). Principals and pastors: Sharing school leadership. *Catholic Education: A Journal of Inquiry and Practice, 5*(1), 85-100.

Brock, B. L., & Grady, M. L. (1995). *Principals in transition: Tips for surviving succession.* Thousand Oaks, CA: Corwin.

Brock, B. L., & Grady, M. L. (2000). *Rekindling the flame: Principals combating teacher burnout.* Thousand Oaks, CA: Corwin.

Brock, B. L., Nelson, L., Grady, M. L., & Losh, M. A. (1998). Public schools and law enforcement agencies: Joining forces for school safety. *Connections, 1*(4), 21-27.

Brock, B. L., Ponec, D. L., Hamman, V., Nelson, L., & Goff, L. (1996). The administration of Nebraska public schools: Present perceptions and future needs. *Educational Considerations, 24*(1), 29-32.

Bruckner, M. (1998). Private lives of public leaders: A spousal perspective. *School Administrator, 55*(6), 24-27.

Bryant, M. T., & Grady, M. L. (1989). Superintendent turnover in rural school districts. *Educational Considerations, 16*(1), 34-36.

Bryant, M. T., & Grady, M. L. (1992). The buck stops here: Critical incidents in school governance as interpreted by superintendents. In M. T. Bryant (Ed.), *Research on school boards and school governance* (pp. 37-49). Lincoln, NE: University of Nebraska–Lincoln.

Carr, A. (1994) Anxiety and depression among school principals: Warning, principalship can be hazardous to your health. *Journal of Educational Administration, 32*(3), 18-34.

Carruth, R. J. (1997, February). *High school principal burnout: A study relating perceived levels of professional burnout to principals' reliance on social bases of power.* Unpublished doctoral dissertation, University of La Verne, La Verne, CA.

Cedoline, A. J. (1982). *Job burnout in public education: Symptoms, causes, and survival skills.* New York: Teachers College Press.

Chance, E. W., & Grady, M. L. (1990). A model for developing visionary leadership. *NASSP Bulletin, 74*(529), 12-18.

Chance, E. W., & Grady, M. L. (1991). *Visionary leadership: Weaving the web and mastering the labyrinth.* Norman, OK: Center for the Study of Small, Rural Schools.

Chaney, R. H., & Forbes, L. M. (1989). Self-concept vs. objective test for Type A/B behavior. *Psychological Reports, 64*(3, Pt. 2), 1115-1119.

Cornett, C. (1986). *Learning through laughter: Humor in the classroom.* Bloomington, IN: Phi Delta Kappa.

Covey, S. (1989). *The seven habits of highly effective people: Powerful lessons in personal change.* New York: Simon & Schuster.

Creagen, E. T. (1999). Healthy habits to avert burnout. *Minnesota Medicine, 82*(8), 14-15, 49.

Dillihunt, V. C. (1986, December). *Stress symptoms and administrative style of urban school administrators.* Unpublished doctoral dissertation, Memphis State University, Memphis, TN.

Domenech, D. A. (1996). Surviving the ultimate stress. *School Administrator, 54*(3), 40-41

DuBrin, A. J. (1997). *Human relations: Interpersonal, job-oriented skills* (6th Ed.). Upper Saddle River, NY: Prentice Hall.

Eckstein, D. (2000). The pet relationship impact inventory. *Family Journal: Counseling and Therapy for Couples and Families, 8*(2), 192-198.

Farber, B. A. (1991, April). *Tracing a phenomenon: Teacher burnout and the teacher critics of the 1960s.* Paper presented at the Annual Meeting of the American Educational Research Association, Chicago, IL.

Fraser, J. M. (1998). *Principal succession in Catholic primary schools in New South Wales: A participant perspective.* Unpublished doctoral dissertation, University of Sydney, New South Wales.

Gallagher, C. (2000). *Going to the top.* New York: Viking Penguin.

Gilligan, C. (1982). *In a different voice.* Cambridge, MA: Harvard University Press.

Gmelch, W. H., & Chan, W. C. (1994). *Thriving on stress for success.* Thousand Oaks, CA: Corwin.

Gmelch, W. H., & Torelli, J. A. (1994, May). The association of role conflict and ambiguity with administrator stress and burnout. *Journal of School Leadership, 4,* 341-357.

Goodman, M. R. (1998, February). *The role of leadership style in the perception of stress among high school principals.* Unpublished doctoral dissertation, Appalachian State University, Boone, NC.

Grady, M. L. (1994). Persistent, pernicious, and perennial: Incidents that lead to superintendent turnover. *Nebraska School Leader, 4*(1), 27-31.

Grady, M. L. (1995a). Creating safe schools: Policies and practices. In K. Lane, M. Richardson, & D. Van Berkum (Eds.), *Safe Schools: What are they? How can I create one?* (pp. 137-160). Lancaster, PA: Technomic.

Grady, M. L. (1995b). *Creating safe schools.* Lincoln, NE: Nebraska Department of Education.

Grady, M. L. (1996). *Rural schools and safety issues.* (ERIC Document Reproduction Service No. ED402121).

Grady, M. L., Bendezú, M. A., & Brock, B. L. (1996). Principals' perceptions of school safety. *Leadership Nebraska, 6,* 18-20.

Grady, M. L., & Bryant, M. T. (1988). *Superintendent turnover in rural school districts.* Charleston, WV: Clearinghouse on Rural Education and Small Schools. (ERIC Document Reproduction Service No. ED308032).

Grady, M. L., & Bryant, M. T. (1990). Critical incidents between superintendents and school boards: Implications for practice. *Planning and Changing, 20*(4), 206-214.

Grady, M. L., & Bryant, M. T. (1991a). School board presidents describe critical incidents with superintendents. *Journal of Research in Rural Education, 7*(3), 51-58.

Grady, M. L., & Bryant, M. T. (1991b). A study of frequent superintendent turnover in a rural school district: The constituents' perspective. *Journal of Rural and Small Schools, 4*(3), 10-13.

Grady, M. L., Haar, J., & Losh, M. A. (2001). The state department of education's role in creating safe schools. In A. P. Goldstein and J. C. Conoley (Eds.), *School violence intervention: A practical handbook* (2nd ed.). New York: Guilford.

Grady, M. L., Krumm, B. L., & Losh, M. A. (1997). The state department of education's role in creating safe schools. In A. P. Goldstein & J. C. Conoley (Eds.), *School violence intervention: A practical handbook* (pp. 58-71). New York: Guilford.

Grady, M. L., & LeSourd, S. J. (December 1989/January 1990). Principals' attitudes toward visionary leadership. *High School Journal, 73*(2), 103-110.

Grensing-Pophal, L. (1999). HR, heal thyself. *HR Magazine, 44*(3), 82-88.

Huberman, M. (1993). Burnout in teaching careers. *European Education, 24*(3), 47-69.

Kijai, J., & Totten, D. L. (1995). Teacher burnout in the small Christian school: A national study. *Journal of Research on Christian Education, 4*, 195-218.

Lennon, P. A. (1992). An investigation of teacher locus-of-control, principal leadership and job satisfaction. (Doctoral dissertation, Seton Hall University, School of Education). *Dissertation Abstracts International, 53* (6-A), 1749-1750.

LeSourd, S. J., & Grady, M. L. (December 1989/January 1990). Visionary attributes in principals' description of their leadership. *High School Journal, 73*(2), 111-117.

LeSourd, S. J., & Grady, M. L. (1991). What is a visionary principal? A research brief. *NASSP Bulletin, 75*(533), 107-110.

LeSourd, S. J., Tracz, S., & Grady, M. L. (1992). Attitude toward visionary leadership. *Journal of School Leadership, 2*(1), 34-44.

Lindberg, A. M. (1983). *Gift from the sea.* New York: Pantheon.

Losh, M. A., Krumm, B. L., Grady, M. L., & Brock, B. L. (1996). Strategies for creating safe schools. *Leadership Nebraska, 6*, 40-43.

McKay, J., & Grady, M. L. (1994). Turnover at the top: Why the superintendency is becoming a revolving door. *Executive Educator, 16*(8), 37-38.

Maslach, C. (1982). *Burnout: The cost of caring.* Englewood Cliffs, NJ: Prentice Hall.

Maslach, C., & Leiter, M. P. (1997). The truth about burnout. San Francisco: Jossey-Bass.

Mind Tools. (2001). Mastering stress for optimum performance. Retrieved from www.mindtools.com/smundstr.html

Nagy, S. (1983). The relationship of Type A and Type B personalities, workaholism, perceptions of the school climate, and years of teaching experience to burnout of elementary and junior high school teachers in a northwestern Oregon school district. (Doctoral dissertation, University of Oregon). *Dissertation Abstracts International, 43* (9-A), 2899.

Payne, R. K. (1994, January). *A study of the relationships among stress resiliency indicators and conflict management styles of school principals.* Unpublished doctoral dissertation, Loyola University, Chicago.

Pigford, A., & Tonnsen, S. (1993). *Women in school leadership.* Lancaster, PA: Technomic.

Ravicz, S. (1997). Distress and eustress among healthy and unhealthy Type A personalities. (Doctoral dissertation, United States International University). *Dissertation Abstracts International, 57* (10-B), 6588.

Schaef, A. W., & Fassel, D. (1988). *The addictive organization.* San Francisco: Harper San Francisco.

Selye, H. (1974). *Stress without distress.* New York: Signet.

Sergiovanni, T. J. (1995). *The principalship.* (3rd ed.). Boston, MA: Allyn & Bacon.

Speck, M. (1999). *The principalship: Building a learning community.* Upper Saddle River, NJ: Prentice Hall.

Stammbach, K. B., & Turner, D. C. (1999). Understanding the human-cat relationship: Human social support or attachment. *Anthrozoos, 12*(3), 162-168.

Stanton-Rich, H. M., & Iso-Aloha, S. E. (1998). Burnout and leisure. *Journal of Applied Social Psychology, 28*(21), 1931-1950.

Taylor, J. D. (1998). *Sisterfriends.* East St. Louis, IL: Quiet Time.

Toy, S. (1998). My fight against depression. *School Administrator, 55*(8), 46.

Whan, L. D., & Thomas, A. R. (1996). The principalship and stress in the workplace: An observational and physiological study. *Journal of School Leadership, 6*(4), 444-465.

Whitaker, K. S. (1995). Principal burnout: Implications for professional development. *Journal of Personnel Evaluation in Education, 9,* 287-296.

Whitaker, K. S. (1996). Exploring causes of principal burnout. *Journal of Educational Administration, 34*(1), 61-71.

Willings, D. (1992). Burnout among teachers of the gifted and gifted adults. *Gifted Education International, 8*(2), 107-113.

Young, B. B. (1998). *Stress management for administrators.* Rolling Hills Estates, CA: Jalmar.

CPSIA information can be obtained at www.ICGtesting.com
Printed in the USA
LVOW011653220911

247438LV00006B/41/P